Enterprise Services Architecture for Financial Services

SAP PRESS

SAP PRESS is issued by
Bernhard Hochlehnert, SAP AG

SAP PRESS is a joint initiative of SAP and Galileo Press. The know-how offered by SAP specialists combined with the expertise of the publishing house
Galileo Press offers the reader expert books in the field. SAP PRESS features
first-hand information and expert advice, and provides useful skills for pro-
fessional decision-making.

SAP PRESS offers a variety of books on technical and business related topics
for the SAP user. For further information, please visit our website:
www.sap-press.com.

Jo Weilbach, Mario Herger
SAP xApps and the Composite Application Framework
2005, 293 pp., ISBN 1-59229-048-5

Forndron, Liebermann, Thurner, Widmayer
mySAP ERP Roadmap
2006, 293 pp., ISBN 1-59229-071-X

Steffen Karch, Loren Heilig et al.
SAP NetWeaver Roadmap
2005, 312 pp., ISBN 1-59229-041-8

Norbert Egger et al.
SAP Business Intelligence
2006, approx. 600 pp., ISBN 1-59229-082-6

Bruno Bonati, Joachim Regutzki, Martin Schroter

Enterprise Services Architecture for Financial Services

Taking SOA to the next level

SAP PRESS

Contents

5 Digging Deeper into Enterprise Services Architecture 41

6 Designing an Application Landscape with Enterprise Services Architecture 59

10 ESA Checklist: The Steps to be Taken   113

A   Glossary   119

Index   123

Foreword

Service-oriented architecture (SOA) is a hot topic. The concept seems to be discussed in every conference, every white paper, and every vendor pitch. Without question, the promise of SOA is alluring: a flexible, adaptable, and affordable IT architecture that supports growth, speed-to-market, and one-to-one customer service. While this rose-colored vision is turning heads in all industries, it's fair to say that it holds special appeal for banks and insurers, who view SOA as a potential panacea for optimizing vintage IT platforms. Based on pure buzz within the financial services industry, SOA seems to have achieved Holy Grail status.

But, as with any other widely hyped phenomenon, it's hard to determine where fantasy ends and reality begins. If SOA is not a Holy Grail, is it at least a pragmatic technology innovation? Is it real, or is it just a marketing mirage—another buzzword to be added to the dictionary of formerly heralded terms and concepts?

SOA: Hype or Holy Grail?

In many ways, SOA is similar to charisma. Everybody has a personal opinion about what it is, but nobody knows how to define it. With SOA, at least, a definition may be agreed on within a given bank, insurer, or technology vendor. But a group that contains a single member is not much of a force. SOA is based on the principles of exchange and interoperability, and these attributes cannot be realized and leveraged if every financial services firm has a unique, private definition of a service-enabled IT environment.

That's the problem this book addresses. If you're new to the world of SOA, these pages cover the fundamentals and principles of service-oriented architecture and, most importantly, its relationship to business issues and business drivers. If you already know a great deal about SOA, you can compare your own understanding with the definition presented herein. Finding these points of agreement and disagreement is important; as we'll learn later on the financial services industry is collectively shaping and refining SOA, and some questions have yet to be answered. If this book serves as a starting point for further discussions within the financial services community, we'll consider that we've reached an important goal.

Who should read this book?

I personally have attended hundreds of meetings with customers, Independent Software Vendors (ISV's) and SAP colleagues where SOA was discussed. In virtually all of these meetings, we reached a point where someone asked, "Are we talking about the same thing?" The answer, up until now, has been, "Not really." That's why I approached two of my associates, Martin Schroter and Joachim Regutzki, and a strategic IT consultant, Bruno Bonati, and asked them to write this book. It probably won't be the last book on this topic, but we have to start somewhere.

To be practical, the authors decided to leverage a real example. Not surprisingly, they use the SAP perspective. And like any bank or insurer, SAP needs to reengineer its core banking and core insurance solutions. Like any bank or insurer, SAP needs to keep legacy solutions running while making step-by-step improvements. And like any bank or insurer, SAP must align IT with business requirements and does not have the luxury of saying, "Hey, listen everybody, let's just put business on hold while we implement a new architecture."

SAP's perspective In a sense, SAP faces the same challenges as any CIO, except that we have hundreds of banks and insurers using our software. This means that interoperability is key; SAP solutions must work flawlessly in many different IT environments. Furthermore, because banks and insurers have the highest possible standards, reliability and maintainability are equally important. Having dealt with all these demands, it could be argued that SAP's perspective on SOA—and on enterprise services architecture (ESA), a more fully realized SOA blueprint—will serve as a good reference point or conversation starter on the benefits of a service-powered IT landscape. This notion has been confirmed in a number of conversations between myself, the authors of this book, and CIOs and chief architects at leading banks and insurers—all of whom have invaluable information to share about their own journey to SOA. On behalf of SAP, I would like to thank them for offering their experiences and insights so freely.

I hope you will enjoy this discussion of the ESA-enabled world. I look forward to future, even more fruitful discussions about how IT can once again become the driver for change and innovation in the financial services industry.

Walldorf, March 2006
Thomas Balgheim
Senior Vice President
Industry Solution Management
Financial Services

1 Global Warming: Stormy Weather Lies Ahead for the Financial Services Industry

Banks and insurance companies have encountered a great deal of turbulence in recent years. Buffeted by far-reaching regulatory change, tidal waves of consolidation, new technologies, seismic shifts in customer behavior, and the globalization of financial functions and capital markets, the traditional structure of the industry has been shaken to the core.

Key challenges for financial services

As a result, the leaders of financial services firms have been forced to ask themselves some profoundly disturbing questions about what their enterprises will look like and how they will succeed in the future. These questions include:

▶ Who are our customers?

▶ Who are our competitors?

▶ What should we sell?

▶ How will we make money?

▶ Where should we be doing business?

▶ What shape should our enterprise take?

▶ How can we grow?

A glance at the business pages of any newspaper or periodical shows that all of these issues are open for debate. On the competitive front, powerful retailers like Tesco and Wal-Mart are tiptoeing (or in some cases, stampeding) into the financial services arena, followed closely by car manufacturers, telcos, Internet services companies such as eBay (PayPal), industrial behemoths like General Electric (GE) and software providers such as Intuit.

Recent trends

Profit margins are also under pressure. Despite a recent history of solid bottom-line results, many financial services firms are wondering how money will be made tomorrow. Insurers are wrestling with a sustained slump in underwriting profits and low investment returns, while banks, which have traditionally relied on a healthy interest rate spread between deposits and loans, suffer from a flat yield curve and mercilessly efficient capital markets, which seem to provide new sources of borrowable money almost at will. In the UK, for example, a feisty middleman called zopa.com uses the eBay model to arrange low-fee loans via the Internet, directly connecting would-be lenders with creditworthy people seeking to borrow money at rates substantially below bank loan averages.[1]

In response, many banks and insurers are calling their organizational structures into question. Despite a longstanding habit of keeping tight control over all corners of the corporation, many financial services firms are looking somewhat enviously at the outsourcing or industrialization model used in other industries, and beginning to ask hitherto unutterable questions about which parts of the organization actually add value and which parts could be better managed by outsiders. An example: Allianz AG, Europe's largest insurer, recently announced plans to create an independent sales company for its German insurance activities.

Viewed historically, trends like these, powerful though they may be, are part of a long history of constant change. Ever since humankind learned to conduct trade with coin and credit (as opposed to clubs and spears) banks and insurers have weathered wave after wave of adjustment and evolution. What is perhaps different today is the actual rate of change. No sooner does a bank or insurance firm make a major decision and craft a new strategy than the environment changes, negating the newly mastered initiative and forcing a new approach.

1.1 Things Fall Apart, and Yet the Center Holds

The foundation of financial services

Still, despite a number of near apocalyptic upheavals and a constant demand for change, no one is suggesting that banks and insurers will disappear, joining former manufacturers of buggy whips, vacuum tubes, and hoop skirts. While financial services firms as we know them may undergo radical modification, there are still some fixed certainties at the center of the financial services business case:

▶ People and businesses will always need to manage their finances.

▶ People and businesses will always need to protect themselves against calamity.

These fundamental truths serve as a source of considerable comfort, even at a time when the future shape of the enterprise is cloudy, barbarians are knocking at the gates, regulators are asking for new risk management controls, and no one quite knows how money will be made tomorrow. When it comes to the financial services organization, however, we should add one final verity:

▶ Banks and insurance companies will always rely on IT to do business.

---

1 "Taking the Bank Out of Banking," *Time*, 10/17/2005, Vol 166 Issue 16, page 29.

1.2   IT as Problem and Solution

An optimally designed and deployed IT landscape is one of the most important tools that a bank or insurer can use to defend against (or profit from) near ceaseless change. Do customers want online, branch-based, and call-center services simultaneously? Does senior management want to complete a cross-border merger and blend operations rapidly so that costs can be reduced? Do product experts want to bundle or unbundle a cornucopia of innovative products so that market opportunities can be seized in a matter of weeks? Have regulators upped the ante by insisting on faster reporting, greater accountability, or new layers of visibility?

In all of these cases, there is little doubt that most banks and insurers see IT as a first line of defense, support, and response. Yet, today's systems, for the most part, remain silo-based—rather good at performing specific chores on behalf of a product line or business unit, but virtually unblendable, incommunicative, and uncooperative across the enterprise. Not only does this result in duplicated systems, data, and processes, but it also results in high expenses, with 80% of most IT budgets dedicated to maintenance, leaving little left over for innovation. Even worse, perhaps, is the fact that today's rather hostile systems make company-wide information hard to assemble, stifle creativity by creating barriers to blended products and services, and hamper mission-critical efforts to set a given enterprise apart from the competition.

Pitfalls of today's IT systems

From an historical perspective, the notion of IT as a barrier is somewhat ironic; in the early days, IT was seen as a powerful driver for change and an enabler of innovation. Lately however, despite the e-business mania of the late 1990s, it can be argued that IT has produced or enabled very little in the way of innovation for financial services companies. In addition to the difficulty associated with integrating systems, processes, and components, another major IT problem has been the lack of reusability. What's missing is a way to separate business processes and application functionality (joined at the hip, since time immemorial) so that either can be changed without causing the other to self-destruct. Over time, any number of IT "breakthroughs" (EAI, object-oriented programming, etc.) have been introduced to address this problem. All have helped. None have succeeded.

1.3 Enter the Service

Web services Though it has been around for some time, the Web service is gaining acceptance as an enabler of integration and reusability in today's IT landscapes. As a freestanding, platform-agnostic, universally accessible chunk of functionality, the Web service has the potential to make all the pieces of the IT landscape play nicely with each other. This helps to explain why service-oriented architecture (SOA), which is already being used by some 40% of European financial services firms according to Forrester Research,[2] is being viewed as something of a panacea for financial services companies who want to extend and improve IT without chopping out the rat's nest and starting from scratch.

1.4 Giving Technology the Business

The enterprise services architecture approach However, despite its problem-solving potential, SOA has not yet proven to be the complete answer for companies that want to modify processes, reuse functionality, and build new, composite applications out of existing resources. While it does help separate business processes from application functionality, SOA, as a generic architecture concept, is necessarily focused on infrastructure. Banks and insurers who have started the SOA journey are realizing that a more holistic viewpoint is needed—one that also includes an evaluation of processes, functionalities, and application architecture. That's why SAP, working closely with many members of the financial services ecosystem, is tapping the laudable muscle of SOA and developing a more robust and accommodating approach known as enterprise services architecture (ESA). As a blueprint for service-based, enterprise-scale business solutions, ESA has the power to help banks and insurers achieve new levels of flexibility and adaptability.

About this book And that, of course, is the premise we'll be addressing in this book. In the following chapters, we'll study the challenges faced by financial services companies, the evolution and role of IT in meeting these challenges, the hope and hype of SOA, and the gathering momentum that's currently propelling ESA to new levels of admiration and acceptance.

But, as you read these pages, remember that enterprise services architecture is a new and evolving concept. For the sake of readability, we write about it as somewhat finite and fully-realized, but the truth is that many forces—SAP, customers, partners, other software vendors, standard-

---

2 *The State of SOA in Financial Services*, by Jost Hoppermann, et al., January 9, 2006, Forrester Research, Inc.

setting groups, and so forth—are part of the mix, and certain ESA characteristics and deliverables may turn out to be different from the present vision. In fact, the journey—like many in IT—will probably never end, as services, business objects, and the architecture that governs them continue to be defined and redefined indefinitely.

Nevertheless, though it may be long, the journey need not be solitary. The very fact that the destination is defined by interoperability and reuse means that there must, perforce, be many other travelers following a similar path. Together, IT providers and financial services companies—competitive though they may be—are working toward shared ideas and principles. Remember, too, that the voyage is just getting underway; thus far, most discussions about ESA and SOA are based on slides, articles, and reports, although early specifications and implementations of some first services are beginning to emerge. That's why this book, admittedly, focuses on current trends and thinking. It is based, in large part, on insights gained by SAP as a leading provider of financial services solutions and a key force behind ESA, but it also draws on the experience gained by banks and insurers who have already started the journey toward a service-enabled landscape.

The journey towards ESA

This speaks directly to the fact that the financial services industry is, in effect, inventing the future of SOA/ESA. Many players are shaping the outcome. Furthermore, as banks and insurers undertake the collaborative journey toward flexibility and adaptability, active, industry-wide participation and cooperation are just as important as inspired landscape design or skillful programming.

Enterprise services architecture requires a new way of thinking. The old "identify the problem and write the code to solve it" approach is no longer valid, if it ever was. Instead, ESA starts with top-down business issues and descends—deliberately, but elegantly—down to the IT level. It requires a new focus on landscape governance, a topic that has been virtually ignored until now. It requires (indeed, it forces) a significant amount of consensus around developing semantics and defining business objects. Moreover, it needs a half-art/half-science methodology for making decisions about how complex or how simple a service should be in order to provide benefits across the enterprise and beyond.

The top-down approach

All in all, this new way of thinking about, designing and managing IT architecture, is neither ridiculously easy nor dauntingly hard. Like many IT endeavors, it works best when done in small steps, which means that ESA can start producing benefits within a very short period of time (some of

One step at a time

these quick wins will be discussed later in this book). The larger prize, for those who commit to the long haul, is substantial: an IT architecture that can help insurance companies and banks meet regulatory challenges, break up the value chain (if so desired), benefit from consolidation, and develop innovative products and services based on customer needs— even if those needs can be satisfied only by crossing traditional boundaries.

But we're getting ahead of ourselves. Let's begin the discussion of how the journey to SOA/ESA can help restore IT's luster, enabling it to become, once again, a driver for change and innovation. To this end, let's move on to Chapter 2, where we'll take a brief look at the fears, features, and forces that banks and insurers must deal with today.

2 The Best of Times, the Worst of Times: A Ping-Pong Game between IT and Business

Are banking and insurance good businesses to be in? Judging by profitability and stock market performance, banks and insurers would appear to be in fine shape. But financial services leaders who look beyond the silver lining see an ominous number of clouds on the horizon, as the trends and conditions are becoming somewhat uncertain. Banks and insurers face an increasingly rigid regulatory environment, a host of emerging competitors, and an uneasy feeling that if they're not growing—organically or via mergers—they're slipping behind their rivals. So, like their counterparts in all industries, financial services leaders are drafting plans to deal with the tough changes and challenges that lie ahead. Invariably, this will mean marshalling IT resources to support new strategies. With this in mind, let's take a look at three fundamental cornerstones that drive the financial services business: reliability, business practices, and growth.

2.1 Reliability

When banking and insurance are compared to other industries, observers often note that it takes too much time to adapt the production landscape to technological innovation. While this claim may have some merit, the sages often seem to forget that the financial services business is marked by special requirements and obligations: banks and insurers manage assets and risks on behalf of individuals, institutions, corporations, and governments. These relationships may last for decades. And they are built on the essential ingredient of trust, which is the very foundation of the financial services business model. To raise the bar even higher, financial services firms must also earn the trust of their partners in the value chain as well as regulatory bodies. If this trust is diminished or impaired, business suffers. If it's destroyed, no bank or insurer can survive.

Adapting to technological innovation

This dependence on trust has a direct impact on what we'll loosely refer to as the production cycle. While most other industries have linear production processes, with a clear beginning, middle, and end, financial services products have longer product lifespans. In addition, cycles may be interrupted or re-triggered as previously sold or contracted products are rolled over, or, as it comes time to deliver the service that a product guar-

The production cycle

antees. As these products and processes change, so do the underlying IT solutions.

If we compare, say, life insurance to automobiles, it's clear that a car manufacturer can more easily adapt production capabilities when shifting from an old model to a new model by setting up a new manufacturing line. For insurers, however, the current capabilities stay in the line for quite some time. Additionally, new financial services products are subject to "on top" innovation; already-sold products must stay in the IT environment—where they require significant administration and monitoring—even as new products are brought to life. This "manage the old while you create the new" approach is hard to master, especially when one tries to do it by enhancing existing IT solutions. That's why banks and insurance companies often decide to introduce additional IT capabilities for new product lines. This practice may eliminate a headache or two, but it has dire consequences; over time, the IT landscape becomes more and more complex.

Compliance requirements Reliability is also important to financial services firms, because they have a strong influence on the economy of a nation. This is one of the reasons why banks and insurers are scrutinized so carefully and why they must deal with stringent, evermore sophisticated regulatory reporting requirements. In Europe, for example, Basel II (not to mention Basel III, IV and V) dictates uniform approaches to risk management for financial services firms. In the U.S., the Sarbanes-Oxley Act (SOX) requires all companies to enhance and certify the processes and activities dedicated to fraud prevention and financial reporting. In all countries, International Accounting Standards (IAS/IFRS) have already had a major impact, while Solvency II looms on the European horizon. Additionally, transactional systems around the world are being subjected to strict compliance standards stemming from laws designed to prevent money laundering, fraud, and terrorism. While it's difficult to forecast future regulatory requirements with any certainty, one clear trend is that banks and insurers will be required to apply highly sophisticated models based on historical as well as current data in order to safeguard the allocation of capital.

IT enhancements From an IT perspective, responding to these pressures will require major system enhancements. While many view this as a costly exercise that creates little real value, it's worth remembering that complying with regulatory requirements reinforces trust, the sine qua non of the financial services business. Those who look beyond the aggravation of compliance may also recognize that reliability can be a strategic advantage. The key is to minimize the compliance-related costs while maximizing efficiency compared to competitors. In the long run, achieving this competitive edge depends on creating a streamlined but powerful IT landscape equipped to manage and integrate all the disparate inputs on which good reporting depends. One specific opportunity in the compliance area is to reduce complexity by fostering better integration of accounting, legal reporting, and internal reporting; better data consolidation and the reuse of functionality in these areas can result in significant cost savings.

Because banks and insurers view reliability and compliance as fundamental cornerstones of their business, they endeavor to support these attributes with highly stable IT environments. Clearly, this is why most financial services firms prefer to stick with proven solutions unless there is a strategic need for change. To avoid risk, IT departments concentrate on small enhancements and minor upgrades rather than wholesale replacements, even when the existing systems are showing their age. This helps to explain why the common call to "break up the value chain" falls on deaf ears in the financial services environment.

All things considered, the attempt to preserve what exists has created complex IT environments for banks and insurers, who now have a mixture of old and new applications and technologies. Ironically, the end result has been the opposite of what was intended; IT has become a source of risk instead of a force for minimizing it.

Where reliability is concerned, the current challenge for IT departments is to create architectures that allow gradual, risk-averse change in order to create an environment that can handle increased regulatory requirements while reducing landscape complexity. The key mandate: *simplify from the inside*.

2.2   Business Practices

The financial services business has traditionally depended on establishing personal relationships between customers and the people who serve them at banks or insurers. In some ways, this approach often serves as a paradigm for financial services IT development. Early IT solutions focused almost exclusively on optimizing internal activities. The goal was to make managers, clerks, controllers and other employees more productive. It was only in the late 1980s, when technologies such as ATMs were introduced, that direct customer interaction became possible. This trend continued with other enhancements like advanced telephony, which powered call centers and other access channels. As a result, banks and

Communication channels

insurers learned, one step at a time, to transfer business processes to their customers. This pleased the customer, and helped create some process efficiency, but it all came about with minimal integration between existing legacy systems and the new technologies.

The Internet era The spectacular rise of personal computing and the emergence of the Internet enabled tremendous change. As people became comfortable with the new technologies, they learned to rely on information from sources other than a trusted loan officer, teller, agent or relationship manager. In addition, electronic intermediaries such as Google, Amazon, and eBay began playing the role of information brokers between consumer and provider. Consequently, in many areas of daily life, the tight integration that previously existed between the customer and his or her financial services provider was replaced by a loose coupling, with service agents mediating access to more and more specialized providers.

Today banks and insurers must woo customers who are quite comfortable using technology to serve themselves. These well-informed, self-confident consumers expect their banks and insurance companies to be just as agile as Amazon, eBay, and Yahoo. With the customer in the driver's seat, it appears that some financial services providers are trying to figure out how to recreate the lost intimacy of earlier days. Some are working hard to develop personalized, customer-centric business processes and information hubs; others are relying on sophisticated tools to analyze customers' behavior and needs. Efforts like these have helped, but they have yet to provide a complete answer. And implementing them, from an IT perspective, isn't easy; very few firms can manage to be truly customer-centric when information is scattered across tightly coupled, silo-like environments. In some cases, the only antidote—expensive though it may be—is the complete replacement of a solution or huge changes to the existing applications; given the strain on IT budgets and the mantra to "do more with less," this option appeals to very few banks or insurers. As a result, IT today faces the question of how to manage change across all applications involved in customer-centric initiatives or other cross-enterprise scenarios.

Increasing complexity Taking a historical perspective, IT has traditionally mirrored business behavior with state-of-the-art development paradigms, languages, and tools. In the early days, the demand was for tightly integrated, monolithic applications that could be operated by power-user employees. Then, with the advent of more and more channels and different user profiles, the solution was to decouple the user interface from business logic, aided by object-oriented development and componentization. Now, in the next round of ping-pong between IT and business, IT departments must come up with architectural models that efficiently support business processes in an environment that is distinguished by loosely coupled consumers and providers. These architectural models will not only have to take care of new applications, but they will also have to accommodate core applications that have been part of the IT scene for decades—such as policy administration, or deposits systems. Yesterday's medicine—building additional new applications—is today's poison. Complexity has reached such a critical level that the IT department must return to its former glory by becoming the *enabler of operational excellence*.

2.3 Growth

Almost without exception, banks and insurers have concluded that basic products and services—loans, deposit accounts, credit cards, health or life insurance, and property/casualty coverage—have become commoditized, with consumers perceiving little difference between competitive offerings. Fred Matteson, CIO of Fireman's Fund Insurance Co., puts it this way: "Competitive differentiation in the insurance industry is like a sailboat race. In a given boat race, all the competitors will be in the same design class, meaning everybody has the same type of boat, the same sails, and the same number of crew members. If you're behind someone, you're going to be behind them until the finish line unless you try something different."[1]

Commodity perception

2.3.1 Growing by Innovation

Perhaps the best way to overcome the commodity perception among customers is to offer differentiated products and services geared to specific customer needs. This attitude is shared across the entire industry. Insurance giants like American International Group, Allianz, or Chubb have launched highly personalized service offerings, and even the smallest players see service as the antidote for commoditization. Improving customer relationships may depend in part on rethinking the branch environment—by extending hours, supplying Internet access, or providing play areas for children—but it also requires new levels of data management and analytics built around state-of-the-art customer information

Making the difference

---

1 Anthony O'Donnell, *Journey to Service-Oriented Architecture*, August 2005, *www.insurancetech.com*.

file (CIF) structures so that customer-facing employees or automated channels can supply the right service at the right time.

Product innovation

Shuffling the product portfolio may be another way to create stronger relationships with existing customers while also attracting new ones. In the U.K., for example, some banks have been offering a bundled account, which contains information on the net interest impact of earnings on deposits and the cost of loans. These products have, by most reports, proven extremely popular with customers, many of whom have shown greatly increased loyalty to their respective banks. Insurance companies, too, are trying to gain a competitive advantage through better-focused products. One example is usage-based pricing products such as "pay as you drive" automobile insurance, with premiums that vary depending on the amount of driving actually done. As a rule, financial services companies want more speed and flexibility when creating new products and pricing schemes, which means that creative ideas for building combined or hybrid products should not be restricted by the boundaries of IT silos. What's needed, in lieu of restrictions, is IT that supports innovative product configuration, price calculation and settlement, with no restrictions on combining homemade products with those of value chain partners.

2.3.2 The Urge to Merge and the Search for New Business Models

Consolidation trends

While banks and insurers maintain a constant focus on organic growth, they also have to contend with ongoing consolidation. The financial services sector appears to be in the midst of an unprecedented era of restructuring—one of the most dramatic consolidations ever undergone by a major global industry. Mergers and Acquisition (M&A) transactions in the financial sector have accounted for approximately half of worldwide merger activity during the last few decades.[2] The consolidation trend shows little sign of abating; many industry leaders appear to have concluded that scaling up can add value and reduce risk while yielding substantial efficiencies. In Europe, where a considerable number of financial services institutions engage in both banking and insurance activities (ING, Fortis, and Dexia, for example), there is a movement toward new business models. One such example is the trend toward forging a collaborative relationship in lieu of an actual merger—with product origination firms working closely with distribution specialists, while intermediaries

---

2 *Mergers and Acquisitions in Banking and Finance*, (Oxford University Press, 2004).

act as a kind of broker between them in order to achieve new levels of efficiency and profitability.

Whatever the approach, the bottom line for IT is that it can either be a major deal-maker or deal-breaker when financial services consider joining forces. Interestingly enough, successful mergers often come with a high-performance IT environment that acts as a consolidation platform, enabling major cost savings down the road. Collaborative models also depend on rock-solid IT so that specialized players along the value chain can maintain a clear focus on core capabilities, with no worries about the ability to integrate into the sales and services network. To summarize, the ultimate requirement of business is that IT should play the role of a strategic weapon, enabling a company to *differentiate successfully on the outside* in order to capitalize on what makes the enterprise unique in the marketplace.

2.4   Can SOA Make It Happen?

In the dynamic financial services business environment of fears, features, and forces described above, many IT departments are struggling to achieve the high levels of agility needed by the enterprise. What's currently required is enhanced flexibility and adaptability—the ability to leverage IT assets in order to cut costs, fend off competitors, push into new markets, and delight customers. Is there a computing paradigm capable of addressing the need to use core systems over multiple geographies, the need for open integration with partners and customers, the need to support new, innovative processes using bits and pieces of legacy systems? The answer, encouragingly, appears to be "Yes." With service-oriented architecture (SOA), a model has surfaced that seems to have the power and flexibility to solve what heretofore has been perceived as an impossible IT problem: how to do more with less.

Flexibility and adaptability

That's the premise, at least. But, like all the approaches and paradigms of the past, one wonders whether SOA will be the next big flash in the pan or the key to creating lasting value within the IT landscapes of banks and insurers. Can SOA deliver on the promise of better reliability, sharper business practices, and healthier growth? Let's find out …

3   SOA: Hope, Hype, or Cold Coffee?

Judging from the number of white papers, chat room postings, Web casts, and newsletter articles, SOA seems to be grabbing a larger and larger slice of mindshare in the IT community. It's been quite some time since an IT architecture topic has received so much attention and debate. Is this obsession justified? Let's perform what is loosely termed a "reality check."

First, as noted above, generic SOA really is an IT architecture topic. It may (or may not) be the way to meet current and future business needs, but it is not a business need in and of itself. It's a fair bet that no C-level executive has ever come to a CIO and said, "What we really need is an architecture built around self-contained, self-describing pieces of application functionality." On the other hand, SOA can definitely be useful when the same C-level executive asks, "How can we shorten our time to market?"

SOA focus

IT departments, software architects, business analysts, and software vendors are (or should be) focused on meeting tomorrow's business needs. Since these are seldom well understood until the last possible minute, flexibility is arguably the most important attribute that an IT landscape must possess. And SOA—which holds out the promise of an easily shuffled and redealt pack of IT capabilities—has the potential to support much higher levels of flexibility than previous technology paradigms.

Business departments don't like to wait. If it takes six months to launch a new IT product (or, even worse, if it takes six months to have a single data field added to a current IT solution), the men and women who control the IT budget are going to become somewhat restless. Yet, despite frustration on both the IT and the business side of the corporate house, it sometimes seems that IT projects continue to get more expensive, take longer to complete, and carry higher levels of risk. Why, despite all the progress made by the business software community over the last 20 years, is IT still such a source of anxiety and frustration?

To answer this question, let's look at two examples. These illustrations will help explain how we have arrived at today's IT impasse, while also clarifying the problem that SOA is poised to solve.

Example 1: the integrated data model

There was a time when IT gurus concluded that the whole world could be mapped in a single data model. Taking this concept even further, the sages suggested that enterprises could use this data model as the base for one "big" application. This credo helped to create the systems that are currently referred to as "monolithic." Solutions built on the "one big application" idea worked very well; they addressed many issues and solved a fair number of problems. (One example would be SAP R/3, the integrated ERP solution that was SAP's flagship product for so many years.)

Over time, however, it became clear that it was quite difficult to accommodate changes and improvements using the single data model. Everything was interconnected. Metaphorically speaking, each little residence in the application neighborhood depended on virtually all of its neighbors. If you wanted to add a new garage to a certain house, contractors had to be sent to every other dwelling in the neighborhood to make corresponding accommodations. Needless to say, this was both difficult and expensive. As a result, the IT departments of financial services companies started to build satellite data models around the central data model, constructing small, dedicated repositories that applications and components could access more quickly and easily. This was a reasonable workaround, but it negated the very premise and promise of integration via one data model. Instead of a single entity, there were now many of them.

Example 2: EAI

In the world of IT, integration has been a problem since time immemorial. At first, the connection problem was solved by point-to-point integration—the linking of two single points via hard coding. This worked fine as long as the number of linked points didn't exceed two. In the real world, however, enterprises wanted to link many points together to meet their IT and business objectives. However, when it came to establishing and maintaining multiple connections, the result was a rat's nest. Every new solution, application, and component created a need for new integration points and the complexity problem worsened by several magnitudes.

The hub-and-spoke model
As seen in Example 1, the integrated data model no longer appeared to be a viable solution to this problem; there simply didn't seem to be any

affordable, elegant way to make old solutions and new solutions work together. So, IT leaders took a new tack by proposing the use of a mediator. If point-to-point integration is unworkable because of its dependence on a cacophony of connections, why not abandon this approach and insert a new layer of intelligence into the technology stack? This master plan is sometimes referred to as a hub-and-spoke model (the hub integrates and the spokes connect to the points that need to be linked), an Enterprise Application Integration Bus (EAI Bus). The fundamental principle is quite compelling; you join each solution or application to one—and only one—central point (the hub). This results in the following benefits:

▶ **Applications do not have to know or understand each other**
The hub serves as a kind of Rosetta Stone, translating both technical languages and the many forms of business slang (i.e., business semantics, and business objects).

▶ **The number of connections decreases**
Because the hub serves as a nucleus, you don't need to make or maintain point-to-point connections between applications and components.

▶ **Changes can be made and managed locally**
Since enhancements are applied at the hub level, they're maintained locally and don't propagate through the network of interconnected applications.

Yet, despite these benefits, the hub-and-spoke model has proven to be somewhat unwieldy. Here's why:

▶ **The demands on the hub's brainpower escalate over time**
"Non-intrusive integration" (the buzzword applied to this model a few years ago) tends to generate the need for a really mighty Quinn. The hub has to understand all the languages spoken in one IT landscape.

▶ **The problem of misunderstanding is pushed to one single place**
The answer for different languages is mapping. The central integration solution gets complicated.

▶ **Point-to-point integration can actually be quite useful in some situations**
Admittedly, point-to-point is not a good approach if the connection between the solutions is built and used exclusively for a single purpose. This is all the more true if the connection hardwires the linked solutions. Yet despite what you may read in Enterprise Application

Integration (EAI) marketing literature, there are times when linking separate points is a good idea. For example, in high volume areas like retail payment, point-to-point connections between the payment application and the disposition tool are a good way of handling the millions of transactions that must be processed within a very short period of time.

Data—
integation—
process

The problems with EAI and the integrated data model help illustrate the central dilemma of IT departments at banks and insurance companies. Financial services firms need IT resources that can be integrated, added to, and reused to meet constantly shifting business goals. The vision has always been to find a way to couple and decouple databases, components, and applications, without locking them into a death grip or creating unmanageable complexity. This can't be done by creating an enormous data model (Example 1), or by creating a new super-smart translation layer (Example 2). Instead, what's needed is a new approach for solving the integration issue—the creation of an architecture that addresses three critical dimensions: data, integration, and process/functionality.

3.1   Getting Back to Basics

IT architecture

When we speak of IT architecture, we're describing the controlled way of conceiving, building, and maintaining a landscape that addresses all aspects required to run a functional system: data, integration, and business processes. Taking a holistic point of view, there are also design, communication, and integration needs that transcend applications, interfaces, middleware, databases, etc., and these, too, can be summarized as architecture. One of the primary goals of IT architecture is to promote better maintainability, to sustain a focus on how well parts of an IT landscape will work together over time, which is something that's often neglected in the rush to complete critically-needed, time-pressed projects. If IT needs are addressed by simply hurling resources at quick fixes and urgent implementations—important though they may be—the overall maintainability of the IT architecture decreases and flexibility is slowly strangled. A quick victory may be won in one area or another, but the concept of reusability (and the resulting fast time to market it supports) is quickly eroded.

Service definition

Service-oriented architecture has the potential to keep IT landscapes supple and flexible, because a key technological ingredient—the service—lies at the very heart of the model. (A service is an exposed, self-contained, and platform-independent piece of functionality with a well-defined interface that can be dynamically located and invoked.)

Services, by their very nature, guarantee that various pieces of software will be forever combinable. To make the picture even brighter, services also ensure that integration issues are addressed up front and not after the fact, as is the case with EAI and most other integration approaches. The integration-at-birth concept is sometimes referred to as "a priori" integration—the opposite of "a posteriori" integration, which happens after a solution or component has been implemented.

The single data model tried to solve the integration problem by creating one mega entity; EAI tried to solve the integration problem by adding a basement after the building was already constructed. Conversely, SOA is inevitably "present at the creation." SOA promotes integration in two key ways. It promotes cooperation at the technology level, because it's based on open standards (with clearly defined rules for messaging, accessing, consuming services, etc.), and because it allows business logic to be decoupled from implementation. It promotes cooperation at the business level, because it emphasizes the use of unified semantics and commonly understood business objects.

Inbuilt integration

SOA is by no means a new idea. The idea and elements (and even software based on them) have been around for quite some time. A good example of an early services-oriented approach is CORBA (Common Object Request Broker Architecture). CORBA allows programs to request services from a server program or object, without having to understand where the server is in a distributed network or what the interface to the server program looks like. While this approach had its merits, and, indeed, is still in use within many IT environments, it did not revolutionize the market and was frequently viewed as overly complex.

Web services and SOA, in contrast, are gaining mindshare, mindset, and traction. Software vendors, software purchasers, and industry observers all seem to be intrigued by the problem-solving potential of a service-powered IT infrastructure. To keep this trend of thinking in proper perspective, however, one should remember that Web services and service-oriented architecture are two different things. Web services are one means of building SOA but definitely not the only one. Moreover, while Web services meet a promising number of urgent needs, they are but one piece of the overall architecture framework.

3.2 So, Is SOA the Answer to the Eternal Quest for Flexibility?

Almost. One of service-oriented architecture's greatest virtues is that it puts integration concerns at the front and center of an application development project. This means that the task of integration undergoes the same design process as that applied to the implementation of functionality. In other words, the integration points are designed as the functionality is conceived, and this occurs prior to implementation. A second significant virtue is that SOA fosters an IT landscape in which business logic can be decoupled from (and made independent of) the underlying technology. Mind you, achieving this somewhat optimistic vision will require broad vendor support, commonly accepted standards, and widespread support for Web service interoperability within the financial services community.

So that's the good news. SOA does have the potential to help insurance companies and banks design and maintain an IT architecture that will help them:

▶ Create new applications on top of existing solutions, increasing the value of current systems and automating new processes while reducing IT costs and increasing efficiency

▶ Meet the IT and business challenges that arise from trends such as globalization, mergers and acquisitions, specialization, and so forth

▶ Adapt business processes quickly thanks to the separation of interfaces and process definitions from the underlying application

▶ Attract new customers by using Web services to improve service, launch new products, and penetrate new customer segments

▶ Solve the multi-channel integration issue

▶ Connect to external partners in order to access expertise, reduce costs, shed asset liabilities, and focus on core competencies—while retaining visibility and control of key processes

▶ Meet compliance requirements more cohesively and cost-effectively

Given these obvious merits, could it be that generic SOA is robust enough to meet the previously described requirements for reliability, business agility, and growth? The answer, alas, is "Not really." As we'll learn in Chapter 4, generic SOA isn't quite powerful enough to make it happen.

4   ESA Overview: Putting SOA to Work in the Enterprise

To gain a better understanding of what service-oriented architecture can and cannot do, let's start with a basic definition:

Definition of SOA

Service-oriented architecture is a software architecture that supports the design, development, identification, and consumption of standardized services, thereby improving reusability of software components and creating agility in responding to change.

A key characteristic of SOA is that it exposes its functionality as services. This promotes near-universal integration, because it allows different applications to easily exchange messages—even if the applications are otherwise incompatible and run in different environments.

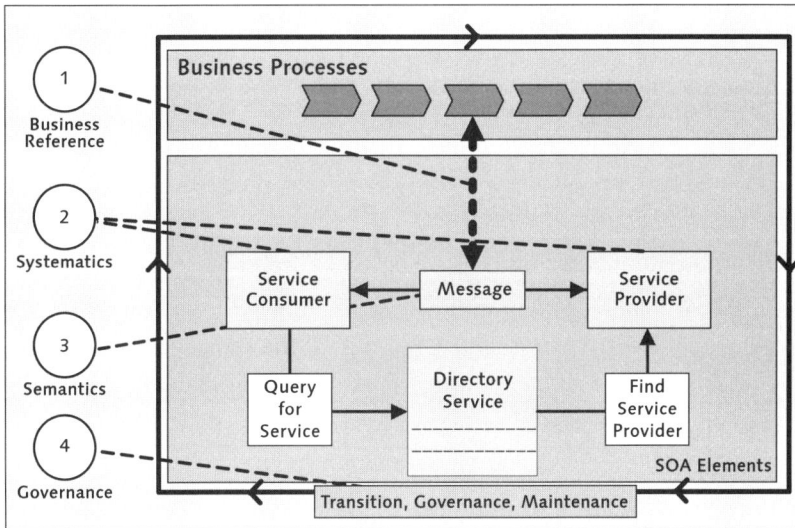

Figure 4.1 Primary Enhancement Needs for Generic SOA

Figure 4.1 depicts service-oriented architecture at its most basic level. At the top, we see a sample business process comprised of several process steps. Directly below, the service infrastructure stands ready to support these processes. The service providers publish a description of their functionality in a directory so they can be discovered and invoked by internal or external consumers. The directory description, too, is based on vendor-agnostic, platform-neutral standards, so that all services are open and accessible to any system, solution, or application. Provider and consumer services communicate via standards-based messaging formats.

Although this model of the generic SOA concept is, admittedly, quite simplified, it helps answer the question most often asked by banking and insurance IT departments (and by SAP as well): Is this simple but flexible architecture robust enough to actually support the things that IT departments and businesses want to do? Or, referring to our figure above, does the services structure in the middle actually support, enable, improve, and enhance the business process layer directly above it?

Challenges for
SOA

The thesis of our previous chapter was that the fundamental principles of service-oriented architecture don't quite ensure the successful use of services at the enterprise level. This is not to say that banks and insurers have been unable to benefit from SOA. A number of diligent and resourceful financial services firms have taken advantage of SOA's core capabilities. However, they have had to solve some thorny IT and business issues along the way. Consequently, there has been a fair amount of discussion and disagreement among IT specialists about the best way of putting SOA to work. These discussions center around four key areas where the pure SOA approach falls short:

▶ **Making architecture relevant to business**
One of the reasons why generic SOA often has problems in business environments is that it doesn't provide an appropriate methodology for the business-specific design of components. This omission creates serious problems for architects and business leaders alike. Without a proper framework for understanding business requirements and addressing them within the IT environment, it is very hard to create the right set of services at a maintainable magnitude.

▶ **Providing a systematic approach for service design**
The basic SOA approach tends to result in the creation of a relatively large number of services. While the services are combinable, the chore of slicing, dicing, and putting them together over and over again, in support of various business processes, is rather cumbersome—similar to building house after house one brick at a time. To be useful at the enterprise level, however, the granularity of services should be determined by the business issues to be solved, and services should be aggregated into components that can be easily reused and maintained. However, it's difficult to determine exactly which and how many service operations should be blended in order to achieve a desired busi-

ness goal. Generic SOA—with its pure focus on IT architecture—provides no guidelines to help with this tricky task.

▶ **Creating a semantic framework**
SOA, as noted above, uses a message-based architecture. Thanks to Web services and XML, there is a widely accepted technical standard available for this messaging. But, even though it's extremely important to communicate openly at the technical level, there is a substantial difference between technical messaging and business messaging, which requires semantic standards, clearly defined business objects, and enterprise- or even industry-wide collaboration to help create them. Also required is the ability to adapt semantics to certain business contexts. Finally, since business objectives and outlooks tend to change over time, it's important that semantics can be adapted accordingly.

▶ **Establishing guidelines for architecture governance, transition, and maintenance**
Successfully implementing SOA at the enterprise level is more than a matter of early testing and piloting activities. To align business and IT infrastructures, a governance model for design, implementation, transition, and maintenance is needed. One of the most important questions here is how to handle subsequent generations of services in order to seamlessly integrate a new iteration of a service into a network of currently running IT solutions. The lack of such a framework in generic SOA approaches explains, in large part, why many projects fail to deliver anticipated results.

4.1   Transforming SOA into ESA

Many early SOA adopters in the banking and insurance communities have experienced the aforementioned problems. In response, they've taken various measures to overcome the issues, and these efforts look quite similar when viewed from an industry perspective. SAP, too, has taken a long, hard look at the inherent strengths and weaknesses of SOA, with an eye toward expanding SOA's architectural focus by augmenting it with business realities. The result is what SAP calls enterprise services architecture (ESA), which elevates Web services into enterprise services by blending them adroitly and combining them with simple business logic to support business processes. This approach is being used not just by SAP, but also by some other early adopters of SOA, based on their real-world experiences.

Adapting SOA to business reality

Just as we did with SOA earlier in this chapter, we'll kick off our discussion of ESA with a basic definition:

> Enterprise services architecture is a blueprint for service-based, enterprise-scale business solutions that offer the increased levels of adaptability, flexibility, and openness required to reduce total cost of ownership. ESA leverages SAP's experience in enterprise applications with the flexibility of Web services and other open standards.

A comparison of this definition and that of generic SOA reveals some fundamental differences, but does not imply that the two architectures are incompatible. ESA embraces the fundamentals of SOA, but adds elements that help financial services companies benefit from the SOA approach at the enterprise level. These elements include not only methodologies for the definition, classification, and implementation of services, but also architectural concepts, paradigms for deployment, and a model-driven design and development approach. Chapter 5 provides details on these topics.

At this point, however, let's briefly expand our understanding of ESA, moving beyond the basic definition presented above to explore a handful of the key characteristics of enterprise services architecture:

▶ **Business-driven design approach**
To successfully introduce a new technology paradigm at the enterprise level, you must have a construction plan. ESA provides a business-driven method for designing and building service-based IT environments. Business-driven means that the processes and requirements of the enterprise serve as the starting point for designing a high-performance, cost-effective IT architecture. Chapter 6 explores the details of this approach.

▶ **Enterprise Services**
As one might expect, the enterprise service is the heart and soul of ESA. Enterprise services can be considered "best practice" services; they support business solutions with just the right functionality at just the right level of granularity—neither too complex nor too simple. Chapter 7 shows how enterprise services are currently being realized.

▶ **Standards and taxonomy**
ESA builds on proven technical standards, using widely acknowledged technical norms, and addressing the need for developing and managing unified business semantics. In Chapter 8, we'll learn why and where standards can provide real value to service-based IT practices.

▶ Transition and lifecycle management

Unlike SOA, ESA provides financial services companies with proce-
dures and guidelines for managing the changeover to a new target
architecture. Although ESA adaptation projects tend to be less labor-
intensive than traditional implementation projects, service-enabling a
complex IT landscape can be a daunting challenge, particularly for
those firms approaching SOA for the first time. Experience and expertise, as always, can pay big dividends here. That's why utilizing best
practices and real-world experience is such an important success factor; not only in the transition phase but also later on, when the service-
enabled IT landscape is exposed to the constant demand for change
that is part and parcel of the business environment. To this end, SAP
and its partners in the ESA community provide a portfolio of valuable
supporting skills. These notwithstanding, the most important contrib-
utor to a successful transition is the internal support and enthusiasm of
IT and business leaders. In Chapter 9, we explore some of the guiding
principles underlying these topics.

4.2   Putting Theory into Practice

Far more than an abstract concept or theoretical design approach, SAP
and the ESA community provide tools and complete solutions, as well as
resources and methodologies to help banks and insurers make the move
to SOA and beyond. Some of these are supplied by SAP and development
or consulting partners. Many others are influenced or will even be provided by banks and insurance companies, who are actively participating
in the community cycles. SAP works with a broad range of industry par-
ticipants to establish and promote mutually beneficial causes. These
include participation in standards-setting groups, sponsorship of business
and IT communities, and support for several other education, training,
and promotional activities. This unfiltered industry feedback is critically
important because it ensures that ESA will remain focused on meeting
business needs.

The ESA portfolio

4.2.1   The Payoff: What ESA Can Do for Banks and Insurers

An ESA landscape is characterized by a number of apparent contradic-
tions: boundaries are put in place (between system layers, between business processes and business applications, and between business objects
and functionality), and yet all of these boundaries are crossable. Solutions, applications, and components are abstracted from business issues,

but not destroyed in the process. The adherence to standards results not in conformity, but in creativity and competitiveness

Service-enabled IT landscapes When all parts of the IT landscape are service-enabled, they're all combinable and reusable; they can be modified according to their own inner circadian rhythms (which are based on the business needs of the enterprise and not on externally dictated release cycles). With a common business language based on mutually accepted semantics and business objects, and a common technology language based on mutually accepted standards, enterprises gain access to a new world of flexibility, adaptability, and speed. Redundancy is eliminated (except where it is deemed to be useful); information flows to wherever it is needed; key capabilities become available across lines of business or product areas; system boundaries no longer define the way banks and insurers do business.

While the journey to ESA is not easy—no worthwhile endeavor is easy—it is something that all financial services companies should consider, because an ESA can help them realize substantial benefits in four key areas.

Reliability and Compliance

Transparency ESA helps to eliminate hidden or redundant data while it fosters the integration of systems and information from all corners of the enterprise. With new levels of transparency and a new ability to assess relationships, exposures, and transactions, ESA supports improved corporate governance and enhanced decision-making. The integration of finance and accounting—traditionally fraught with resistance and conflict—becomes much easier to accomplish. With better views of the information in legacy systems, multiple instances, and subsidiaries, ESA gives financial leaders powerful resources for meeting the requirements of Basel II (or III, IV and V), International Accounting Standards (IAS/IFRS), Solvency II, Sarbanes-Oxley Act (SOX), and other compliance or regulatory bodies.

Example: As is true today, it is very likely that an ESA-enabled enterprise will still operate many different systems in order to support its daily business activities. This means that in order to create the required reporting data, the enterprise will still have to cull data from many different sources; however, there are two reasons why this compliance task will be easier in an ESA-powered environment. The first has to do with business semantics; a reporting requirement imposed by a regulatory body can be understood as the origin of a compliance request.

SAP NetWeaver Business Intelligence has configuration capabilities that allow modeling of the required reporting output in a flexible way, making the source data available via appropriate enterprise services to valuation tools such as those provided by SAP's integrated finance and risk architecture (IFRA) framework. The other way in which ESA helps with compliance has to do with technical integration; here, ESA provides concepts and tools for the seamless integration of information sources and target systems, thereby handling all relevant requirements such as performance and security.

Consolidation and Cooperation

Because it results in combinable, integrateable processes and applications, ESA is an ideal support mechanism for banks and insurers who want to join forces with competitors or partners in the value chain. Economies of scale—instead of being distant mirages—are actually attainable. Thanks to the transparency and openness of ESA landscapes (which reduce or eliminate the hidden hard-coding that is such an impediment to change), merged or acquired units can be blended quickly so that cost savings flow to the bottom line as early as possible. Differing sector standards such as the Single Payments Area for Europe (SEPA) initiative can be navigated and accommodated more easily, and system landscapes can be optimized to meet the strategic and operational needs of the cooperating entities.

Open landscapes integration

Example: The ESA model helps banks and insurers create a unified landscape for different areas of business responsibility: sales and service, operations and execution, business support, and so forth. Once a unified IT landscape with clearly defined responsibilities is in place, the potential outcomes of both—M&A as well as cooperation decisions—can be evaluated more easily because the number of possible scenarios is reduced. ESA also promotes "inbuilt integration," as we'll learn in Chapter 5. This results in a landscape that is, by definition, prepared to integrate with others, thereby reducing the incompatibility that has been so problematic for many mergers.

Enabling Differentiation and New Business Models

ESA, with its "integration-from-the-beginning" paradigm, gives process owners and business leaders control and oversight of any in-house or outsourced business process. As processes become standardized, simplified, and scalable, a wide range of new strategic options becomes available.

Shared information

Example: Natural, frequent catastrophes like earthquakes and hurricanes pose a risk not only to their victims, but also to financial services firms. Today, banks and insurers have a great deal of information about houses, buildings, and other properties that may be affected by a disaster. With an ESA-enabled IT landscape, enterprise services can be used to augment and combine this data with information on weather, location, and relevant facts. This would not only allow banks and insurers to evaluate damage once a disaster has occurred, but also to proactively consult their customers on how to protect themselves and their property in the event of a natural disaster. Equally important, such capabilities would help to facilitate collaboration and teamwork between partners along the value chain, such as businesses specializing in disaster-recovery or protection services.

Customer Intimacy and Innovation

Process innovation

With ESA, IT is no longer a bottleneck. Service-driven applications provide an endlessly malleable foundation of functionality to support current or newly created processes. Speed to market improves; dynamic pricing and servicing options can be created to meet the needs of customer segments in quantities as small as one. Instead of making decisions based on product boundaries, channel restrictions, system silos, or a line of business rivalries, decisions can be made based on the value of the idea itself.

Example: Today, many banks and insurers want to offer products with prices that are based on the degree to which a customer uses them. One example is "pay as you drive" auto insurance, with rates linked to mileage, but the idea applies equally well to auto leasing. Today, the required data is often collected in traditional, somewhat labor-intensive ways. With ESA, banks and insurers could use the capabilities of SAP NetWeaver to automate the data collection process by receiving mileage information electronically from external sources—which might include a hub that gathers information from car service providers or "mileage black boxes" in the cars themselves. Once available in the SAP NetWeaver Business Intelligence environment, an enterprise service will consolidate the data and feed the mileage information into a configurable pricing engine that computes the premium to be paid by the policyholder or lessee. Additional steps could include invoking appropriate enterprise services in contract administration and invoicing in order to trigger the required update to the contract, while also initiating the premium collection process. From this point, additional enterprise services could bring the overall process to its logical conclusion by automatically creating the required entries in the general ledger and the cash forecast system, while also performing tasks such as generating and delivering statutory reporting information.

4.3   The Changing Role of IT

Just as enterprise services architecture dictates a new way of looking at governance and development issues, it also forces a reexamination of the role of IT and of IT management. ESA, as we've seen, begins with business requirements and not with architecture, systems, or applications. The impact on IT is quite similar. The role of IT managers evolves, in effect, from that of second level management to the boardroom. No longer an order taker or process facilitator, today's CIO must be a strategic thinker. (As if this idea needed any further proof, it's no longer a novelty when a CIO becomes CEO in today's information-driven business environment.)

The role of IT managers

One way of categorizing this heightened role and responsibility is to regard IT executives as portfolio managers who must help make strategic decisions about running the areas under their supervision. Since pure architecture projects haven't traditionally been showered with budget resources, IT leaders must develop diplomatic and collaborative skills at levels that would have been unimaginable only a few years ago.

ESA, while it offers tremendous upside potential, cannot be treated as just another IT initiative. When Credit Suisse, for example, began to pursue SOA objectives, the IT department made the radical decision to put its entire budget allocation in one neutral pot. Under the leadership of the CFO, a board—consisting of senior IT and business leaders—was established to govern the flow of funds to worthwhile business and IT projects. This avoided the "squeaky wheel gets the grease" allocation approach, reserving funds for longer-term, holistic projects such as the definition of business objects and the development of reusable services. Bruno Bonati, the then-CIO, notes that the organization of Credit Suisse's IT department changed fundamentally as the need and value of SOA came into focus. "Everything had to be organized around SOA," he says. "We needed new skills, new processes for provisioning, for versioning, and for enforcing the reuse of services. But, above all, we found we had to manage everything with an architectural focus—which was quite a change for us, and for any IT department."

An example

Summary: ESA is an architecture that addresses all three requirements of a future-proof IT landscape: data management, integration, and support for flexible, adaptive business processes and functions. With enterprise services architecture, IT is no longer the problem but the solution—or, at least an enabler of the solution. A final thought, as we move on to a greater exploration of key ESA issues, is that with enterprise services architecture, IT becomes a strategic weapon instead of a necessary but somewhat maddening colossus.

5 Digging Deeper into Enterprise Services Architecture

An enterprise service is an industrial strength Web service. Enterprise services architecture is service-oriented architecture on steroids. Though these phrases are, of course, non-technical and somewhat fanciful, they capture the core distinction between these evolving software models. Web services are extremely useful—and becoming ubiquitous—but they don't quite support all the things that a bank or insurer must do to survive and thrive in today's fluid, tempestuous environment. Web services do a single thing very well. However, they are so finitely focused and so granular that it's hard to efficiently corral enough of them to support business processes. The solution? Combine clusters of Web services with business logic into enterprise services so that important decisions about how to blend and combine them have already been made.

When a business agreement is signed (for a new deposit account, insurance policy, etc.), a service can be used to transfer the agreement into the operational solution of a bank or insurer. In the real world, however, signing a contract tends to have consequences. It almost always generates other actions that must be performed—such as notifying credit agencies, calculating compensation for sales personnel, updating customer collateral, or calculating net present value. With ESA, the supporting business logic can be shaped so that all these actions happen in concert. Thus, ESA is not only service-driven, it's also event-driven. Enterprise services architecture is a blueprint that fully realizes the SOA vision as a comprehensive architecture for the next wave of business software.

Service-driven and event-driven

In this chapter, we'll look at the ways in which ESA improves on SOA. We'll also try to bring the architectural model of ESA into sharper focus. This is an important topic. ESA and SOA are based on similar principles, but ESA goes considerably further by putting theory into practice. Generic SOA is naked architecture; ESA is architecture with business brains. ESA provides a blueprint for real-world implementation; SOA does not.

ESA is a consistent architectural concept with a clear implementation roadmap; it supports functionality that integrates easily into business contexts. This last point is especially relevant for banks and insurers, who manage large data volumes and depend on tight integration between processes that are linked by recurring events and common start points.

As we expand our understanding of enterprise services architecture, we'll examine the following ESA-related concepts:

▶ Understanding an enterprise service as a contract

▶ Model-driven architecture

▶ Communication paradigms

▶ Service providers and consumers

▶ Service implementation

▶ Deployment

5.1 The Enterprise Service as a Contract

Who owns the services? A Web service is a freestanding, platform-agnostic, standards-based chunk of functionality. Self-contained and self-describing, it can be found and accessed by applications (usually called consumers) using a universal language for discovery, description, and delivery of whatever it does. Looking beyond this basic definition, it's helpful to remember that a service, by nature, has aspects of a contract. This contract is not a binding covenant in the legal sense, but an implied agreement between the consumer of a service and the provider of a service. The contract defines the common language (semantics), the functional behavior, and any necessary non-functional aspects that govern the uncovering, messaging, and utilization of functionality. In essence, a service contract states, "As long as you play by the rules, I promise to do some work for you." To support this implied understanding, a service's semantics and functional behavior should be independent from the implementation (the actual coding), and therefore independent from the service provider.

But, to achieve this autonomy, you must answer a very important question: "Who owns the service and defines the contract?"

There are two basic responses to this query. We'll call them models:

▶ The provider owns the service and defines the contract.

▶ A central, logical instance owns the service and defines the contract.

5.1.1 The Provider Model

Default Web services The provider model is the default approach for a pure Web service technology stack (one comprised of WSDL for the description language, SOAP for specifying transport parameters and UDDI for communicating how to advertise and discover the service). With the provider model, a developer writes an interface and publishes it as a WSDL description in a UDDI directory. A potential consumer can browse the directory at any time. If the consumer finds something useful, the Web service is selected and then implemented. In this scenario, it's clear that the provider shapes and offers the implied contract, basically saying, "Here's what I'm offering; take it or leave it." The consumer can accept or decline the contract but there is no negotiation or collaboration between the two parties as to what the service should or should not do.

5.1.2 The Central Model

The central model, which ESA builds on, uses a higher-level architectural perspective. In a somewhat radical departure from today's norms, the contract is defined *prior* to the writing of the interface and the actual coding. Stakeholders representing the provider and consumer get together (in a virtual sense) and say, "Let's figure out what we want to do and then build functionality that will help us do it." Theoretically, a contract could be designed without having any actual providers or consumers in mind. As a rule, however, contract definitions are more often triggered by the need to support actual business or IT scenarios, with potential providers and consumers known up front.

The provider model has its good points. It solves some of the problems associated with current application landscapes by helping to support the integration of heterogonous technologies, and by enabling the separation of interface definitions and implementations. However, the provider model comes up short as a foundation for service-oriented architecture, because it creates too much variation in semantics. As previously explained, providers determine semantics in most of today's landscapes. This creates an annoying situation in which various components and applications use different meanings for what should be a singular object (customer, contract, payment, debit, etc.). This Tower of Babel situation arises from the fact that the underlying implementation of a provider is what dictates the semantics associated with the service.

This problem has resulted in a great deal of painful, expensive, point-to-point integration. Enterprise application integration (EAI) has been—and still is, to a certain extent—a fairly effective antidote. EAI creates a central, intermediate instance that knows how to translate the different semantics from one component to another. This definitely improves point-to-point integration, but it doesn't solve the problems associated with having many different semantics throughout the IT landscape.

EAI: central and painful

Another problem with EAI is that someone has to keep track of what goes on within each EAI link, maintaining an understanding of how information from point A is translated as it makes its way to point B.

Of course, an enterprise could simply declare that all consumers must accept provider-supplied semantics. (We'll call this the "Do it my way" approach.) This would force consumers to map their locally used semantics to those of the provider. While this would relieve the central EAI challenge, it would obviously not lead to a unified language based on a common semantic structure. With no harmonization of the meaning of verbs and phrases, each consumer would be forced to understand many meanings for the same word—akin to a multilingual translator who happens to know the word for "contract" in 87 different languages.

5.2   Defining the Right Semantics

A single source of truth

Ironically, the "Do it my way" approach also applies, in a sense, to the central model; here, consumers and providers are *both* forced to accept a common semantic structure. However, the outcome is more beneficial, because now there is a single source of truth about semantics, which means that all the people and all the applications within an enterprise (and, ideally, beyond) accept the same definition for key concepts such as "sale," "account," and "address." To be sure, a certain amount of local translation is still required on the consumer end, but this is kept to a minimum. Following the object-oriented principle of hiding the inner details of providers, the central model generalizes low-level minutia into a common language.

The meaning of semantics

At this point, we'll digress briefly in order to discuss the concept of semantics. Strictly speaking, semantics is the study of meaning—a science that delves into the concepts and connotations associated with a given word. Take the word "desk," for example. The word itself is obviously "desk," but the *meaning* of these four letters strung together in this particular order is, "A piece of furniture with a writing surface and, usually, with drawers or other compartments." In computing, the same sort of association is made between a word and its meaning, except that from a coding perspective, the meaning will necessarily be quite precise, expressed in various bits and bytes, formats and formulae, depending on the programming language. Another key distinction here is that unlike a spoken word, the meaning of which is beyond the control of any single person or group, software words can mean whatever an enterprise wants them to mean. The problem, up until the advent of ESA, has been that different parts of the organization have assigned different meanings to the same word—which makes it very difficult to integrate applications or create new ones based on previously installed components.

With enterprise services architecture, the semantic structure has an implicit hierarchy. Semantics are defined at several levels, the lowest of which is words or verbs, which are known within SAP as global data types or GDTs. Examples of GDTs are "name," "account number," and "agreement." While a certain amount of effort is required, it's a relatively simple matter to define the attributes of a word, which would include its length and meaning. In the aggregate, these words become the semantic vocabulary of an enterprise and a basis for describing business objects and defining the phrases (or messages, technically speaking) that are exchanged by consumers and providers.

The next level in the ESA semantic hierarchy consists of business objects and contracts. Comprised of (or built on) words and verbs—business objects and contracts are broader, but equally precise. An example of a business object is "account" or "customer." An example of a contract is "credit check" or "account creation request."

5.3   Little Drops of Water, Little Grains of Sand

Thanks to standards-based protocols, services make communication and messaging relatively easy. However, the way that communications happen will vary, because consumers and providers need different things at different times. For some relatively simple tasks, the conversation must be interactive, immediate and based on short sentences (i.e., "Save this document." "OK, it's saved."). At other times, communication is based on a mail-style exchange, where a consumer asks for something more complicated (i.e., "Please analyze this customer data to see how many customers with life insurance policies also have auto insurance with our company." "OK, I'll do it and get back to you later.").

In measuring the complexity of a service, the term "granularity" is often used. Fine-grained services are simple; coarse-grained services are complex. This is based, in part, on the fact that services tend to fall into two basic groups.

Granularity

The first group consists of relatively simple, generic services that link directly to a business object. These are known—somewhat unfortunately—as CRUD (Create, Retrieve, Update, and Delete) services and they are typically employed within a user interface—a place where one

CRUD services

needs fast, synchronous communication, with small increments of inter-action.

The second major group consists of services that support business docu-ments. These, in turn, fall into two major categories:

▶ Interactions between consumers and providers across company bor-ders (often called B2B or business-to-business)

▶ Interactions between consumers and providers within an application landscape (sometimes called A2A or application-to-application)

If the goal of a bank or insurer is to create sufficient flexibility to break up the value chain, this distinction would be irrelevant. Landscape-specific messages wouldn't be used; instead, messages would be based on B2B standards exclusively. But, for this to be possible, all messages exchanged between industry-wide entities would have to be based on mutually accepted standards. While financial services companies are working hard to develop universal standards, an all-B2B environment remains some-what elusive at present.

Yet, even though it's difficult to imagine all banks and insurers adhering to universally accepted norms, A2A universality within the enterprise is quite possible. Messages (and the contracts woven into them) can be standardized so that they are instantly comprehended within the far reaches of an organization. That's what ESA is all about.

Conclusion: Because ESA creates an IT landscape based on common semantics, the difficulty of semantic integration is virtually eliminated. ESA creates a common language—a kind of Esperanto[1]—so that any translation happens locally, without the need for a ubiquitous transla-tor. With processes and applications built around commonly accepted business objects, banks and insurers can reduce complexity, enhance efficiency, and lower costs.

5.4   Model-Driven Architecture

Sooner or later, the term "separation of concerns" will arise in any discus-sion of software architecture. This is by no means limited to newer approaches like SOA and ESA; it has always been an essential part of design and runtime. A good example is the separation of presentation

---

1   Esperanto is the most widely spoken constructed international language.

logic and business logic; this division enables independent lifecycle management, which means that developers can make non-propagating changes in either of the two areas. In other words, to a large extent, it's possible to change the look, feel, and order of user interfaces without impacting the underlying business logic.

Separation of concerns is also important when designing business applications. The designers must clearly specify what functionality will or will not be provided, and what data will or will not be known. It's also important to determine what will be provided and what will be consumed. (Yes, this discussion has now spilled over into the world of services!) Services, by nature, integrate rather easily. But they also have the ability, or tendency, to keep things separate. Thus a service not only brings a consumer and a provider together, it also separates them from each other. This is similar to the familiar rhetorical question concerning brick walls: "Does mortar keep the bricks together or keep them apart?"

5.4.1 The Border Patrol

To a certain extent, defining borders depends on your point of view. Let's examine this idea in terms of the two service models (provider model and central model) that we just discussed:

Focus on borders

▶ The provider model primarily emphasizes integration (though separation is explicitly available as well).

▶ The central model primarily emphasizes separation, since defining a contract means defining a border simultaneously.

To dig into this concept a bit more deeply, let's consider the example of a service that provides the current balance in a comprehensive customer account. This provider, in turn, is a consumer for other providers who supply data on balances of various sub accounts owned by the customer in question. Clearly, the comprehensive balance—as well as information about various assets and liabilities—should be provided in a single currency, even though some of the holdings may be denominated in foreign currencies. This means that currency conversion will be required, and it can be done in one of two ways. Either the service providers will be indifferent to the requested currency, and always provide balances in the originating currency, or the service providers will be asked (or forced) to do the conversion before supplying data. How this is handled is relatively unimportant. What is important is that the messaging between consumer and provider clarifies the decision about where the conversion should be done.

An example

Until now, drawing well-defined borders has not been a primary or popular architectural activity. In the monolithic mainframe applications which are typically used by banks and insurers today, the idea has been to provide an integrated solution in "one box." Decisions about currency conversion between components were made (along with thousands of other conclusions), but they were hard-coded into the landscape, where they now remain somewhat buried: hard to find and hard to change. This, in turn, makes ongoing integration something of a headache, if not an impossibility. It also helps to explain why banks and insurers have not jumped on the outsourcing bandwagon; in light of high IT integration costs, the business case hasn't made much sense.

5.4.2 The Very Model of a Modern Major General

Model-driven architecture Drawing borders, far from being a low-priority nuisance, is one of the most important things a bank or insurer must do to take advantage of the new service-powered world of software architecture. In recognition of this principle, ESA features model-driven architecture (typically known as MDA). The basic idea is that system functionality is defined as a platform-independent model, using an appropriate specification language, and then translated to one or more platform-specific models for the actual implementation. This creates an architecture that is neutral with regard to language, vendors, and middleware.

With ESA, architects look at service definition and service borders simultaneously (indeed, they have no choice but to do so). Not only does this ensure the utmost flexibility and adapdability going forward, it also means that you don't have to live with the consequences of a bad decision. In other words, if you define a contract without thinking of the consequences in terms of borders, the result could be painful. Imagine an automobile in which the engine tried to do some of the steering, or the transmission tried to do some of the braking. This would be inefficient at best, fatal at worst. In the world of IT, however, the consequence is not a life-threatening car crash, but the aggravating expenditure of time and money needed to fix the problem. One of the primary benefits of MDA is that it promotes and manages the establishment of borders, which means you won't have to take your IT landscape to the dealer for an expensive tune-up or repair job.

5.4.3 Border Wars

Most software solutions are made up of many components. The component with the finest granularity is the class/object in Java and ABAP, or the function module in other programming languages. The key question for a bank, insurer, or any company interested in leveraging ESA is how granular a component should be. Small, discrete, and infinitely flexible? Or large, compounded, and targeted to a specific functionality and process? This is a watershed decision that will affect the ultimate usefulness and value of any SOA or ESA landscape.

Granularity of components

▶ If the granularity of components is too fine, a certain amount of flexibility is gained, but a price is paid in terms of high performance overhead.

▶ If the granularity is too coarse, flexibility diminishes and it becomes harder to build new applications quickly, or break up the value chain.

To address this challenge within ESA, SAP supports a bidirectional model for setting the right granularity. This is quite different from the so-called "waterfall" model, where architects model one architectural level and then proceed down to the next, more detailed level. Instead, ESA uses a kind of oscillating approach; architects move back and forth between the different levels of models and definitions. This means that architects start by designing borders based on process needs and process understanding. Next, they decide on the right level of granularity using a kind of enlightened trial and error process—with the pendulum swinging back and forth between flexibility and efficiency—until the right balance is found. While this process may sound time-consuming, it produces highly beneficial results because it unites business's demand for flexibility with IT's demand for stringent development processes.

Oscillating approach

5.4.4 Flexible Components

ESA also enables a flexible deployment of software components (which, in turn, supports highly flexible processes). The first step in designing components is to define borders and interfaces, and you begin this process by looking at the highest-level business objects— those that have the most global acceptance within an organization. The high-level model— which may be a grouping that includes, for example, 10 to 12 simpler business objects—is outlined and detailed, and then can be cut into various pieces that support specific business processes or concerns. Similarly, software components that will do the actual processing are sliced up and linked to the appropriate business objects.

Borders and interfaces

To reinforce this concept, let's briefly review these first steps in a model-driven architecture:

▶ Identify the high-level business objects needed to support an enterprise's business processes.

▶ Specify which lesser objects within the high-level group should be aggregated to achieve a desired result.

▶ Determine where borders are necessary or possible.

▶ Map and link software components to the business objects so that the new vehicle will actually run when the key is inserted into the ignition.

▶ Tweak and shift borders (or detach business objects) if improvements or changes are called for.

This is very similar to the process used in data modeling; you start with a normalized version of a specific model and then de-normalize or shift borders as needed.

Public borders (those that describe what is exposed by a component) are defined by the contracts drawn up using the "central model" we described at the beginning of this chapter. In MDA, these public borders must adhere to the global model. When it comes to a component's internal structure, however, providers and consumers are free to draw their own maps; this makes sense—since inner implementation is also up to them. This means that a provider is free to build functionality in an object-oriented language, or any other procedural language. Once built, the resulting components will encapsulate one or more business objects. They will also assume responsibility for maintaining the consistency of the business object within an instance, and for providing any process knowledge that may be reside in the component.

Example for separation of concerns

Let's now look briefly at an example of what happens when borders are established, a process sometimes referred to as "separation of concerns." When it comes to creating a printout of account statements, for instance, a bank may want to have one central output management system (OMS). Along with its other duties, the OMS must ensure that correct formats and layouts are applied to the print output. However, the OMS is typically not responsible for taking required input data such as account balances, postings, or address data. Therefore, to produce the print output, the OMS must consume services from other systems, such as a deposits system for account-related information or a customer information system for address data. In the ESA environment, part of the border definition process would be to determine which services in these other systems should be responsible for delivering the information, along with exactly how the information should be delivered. This resolution is reflected in a clear assignment of responsibilities among the systems, as each system performs specific tasks without duplication or conflict. These responsibilities are also visible at the outer layer of the systems through the functionality that the services expose in their interfaces. In other words, enterprise services create clear centers of responsibility, each of which works on different tasks and/or business objects.

5.4.5 Location, Location, Location

Speaking of process knowledge, we have now advanced to another interesting endeavor, albeit, one that is greatly enhanced by MDA. When designing an architecture, it has traditionally been difficult to choose the software layer in which process knowledge should reside. (Traditionally, the three primary choices are the presentation or user interface layer, the business process layer, and the layer within applications and business objects.) Some of these decisions are relatively easy. For example, business logic regarding consistency should be located directly with the business object itself. However, it's harder to determine what a software component must know about a process, and whether this knowledge should be maintained in the process layer via a Business Process Management (BPM) tool (an instance to handle process flows centrally) or in the user interface layer.

Software layers

The main difference between these two possibilities is that providing local component knowledge is more straightforward. That's because BPM tools usually follow a request/reply model with their providers. If knowledge about follow-up steps, or even complete subprocesses, is available locally at the UI level, it's much easier to use a fire-and-forget (or "one call") mechanism instead of the request-reply (or "two call") protocol needed for BPM tools.

BPM tools

MDA is different from previous approaches like enterprise resource modeling or object-oriented modeling, because it accurately reflects all potential providers and consumers. This behavior is feasible because the implementations of providers and consumers are derived from business object models. From a high-level point of view, this is enabled by the extensive use of the "interface concept," which is employed in object-oriented programming.

The contract (as discussed in Section 5.1) is described by an XML schema. This semantic contract—which defines the business elements of a ser-

Interfaces

vice—is used to generate an interface for a specific environment like ABAP or Java. In these environments, the term "interface" is used in the context of object-oriented programming, meaning that while it is first available in an environment-specific language, it still has to be implemented into the specific software component (in Java, the key word for this is "Implements"). However, the term "interface" actually applies only to the provider; the consumer implements a proxy or, in pattern language, a façade.

When working with the object model, you must specify the details that have to be known during modeling. Any information exchanged across software components must be specified within the vocabulary of the global semantics or language. Therefore, the global semantics are an intra-component conversation language. Elements and entities known only locally don't need a global name.

5.4.6 Reflecting on Reflections

Model reflecting implementation

As stated earlier, with MDA the model reflects the implementation and vice versa. At first blush, this may sound counterintuitive. Most developers and architects know from past experience with modeling that models reflect implementation only at the very beginning of the design process; later on, they diverge. Sometimes massively.

To prevent this anarchy, you must link the higher-level models of the business objects, service definitions, and software components to the actual implementation. Furthermore, this linkage must be binding; when change is needed, adjustments must be made in the model first, implementation second. This does not contradict the fact that a model is an entity; it might exist with one or several concrete implementations or with none. Where implementations do exist, the model describes all their visible parts and none of these parts can be changed in the implementation alone. Remember however, that this rigidity ultimately allows flexibility; changing a service—even on the attribute level—often shifts a border or assigns a specific business functionality to another software component.

Interlinked models

From a modeling tool perspective, this implies that the different models —business process models, technical process execution models, object models, and the like—are interlinked, and you can easily navigate from a high-level overview down to implementation and back up again. You should note, however, that the modeling tool alone does not solve all the design issues and that "A fool with a tool is still a fool." In addition to modeling methodologies and a good understanding of business issues, a healthy amount of control, oversight, and governance is necessary to design a service-powered IT landscape.

Although it's wise to follow a strict model first approach, this does not mean that the implementation is completely dependent on the model. Modeling addresses the visible elements and therefore the "model first" approach is valid for only these parts. This means that implementations can have their own various internal and non-visible parts and details. It also means that two implementations of the same model can be quite dissimilar. Remember that, as was stated earlier, the inner implementation is left to providers and consumers, which means that you can use MDA to build services over an existing application.

The model first approach

Conclusion: Using model-driven architecture—a key feature of ESA, but not of SOA—you always have an up-to-date description of your IT landscape, with well-defined borders. Not only does this give you a clear picture of who is providing services and what the services do, it also makes it easy to drill down for a more detailed view. This makes it a relatively simple matter to understand and analyze the impact of any changes.

5.5   Communication Paradigms

Decoupling—or loose coupling—is a primary characteristic of enterprise services architecture. This means that business objects, though they will always be linked in some ways, can be quite independent from each other and that the different software layers (primarily the application integration layer, business process layer and presentation layer) are similarly untethered. A primary benefit of decoupling is that a given software component becomes largely independent from other linked components and therefore, it can be introduced, upgraded, or retired according to its own self-determined lifecycle. In addition, allied components can also be swapped, as long as the new version sticks to the same contract(s). A third advantage of decoupling is that it makes changing possible routes of a process considerably easier.

Benefits of decoupling

On a business and technical level, the highest level of decoupling is achieved when a message is sent from a consumer to a provider and no immediate answer is expected. This is known as asynchronous communication; one software component sends a message and, without waiting for an answer, finalizes its local work assuming that a certain outcome will ensue. The receiver acts on the incoming message and has to ensure a proper handling of that message. (Lower levels of functionality ensure that the message is sent in the appropriate service quality.) The provider does not have to take responsibility for the message delivery, or for any technical errors that might occur "on the wire."

Forward error recovery

This is generally known as forward error recovery. It means that a receiver will be obliged to take care of possible business situations that may arise when a message is accepted. A good example of forward error recovery can be found in the process of handling payments across multiple organizations. In virtually all financial services companies, debits and credits take place more or less constantly, at many different times and places; however the payment order is not complete until debiting and crediting are reconciled. Sometimes, however, this process is less than smooth; a "sender," for example, might debit an amount that has to be canceled later on. With forward error recovery, managing this cancellation is handled by the receiver.

Asynchronous vs. synchronous communication

With asynchronous communication, there is *no* blocking call in place. With synchronous communication, there *is* a blocking call in place and the consumer waits for a response from the provider before acting locally. This does not imply that you can't exchange information via messages. In fact, most SOA frameworks use messages for both asynchronous and synchronous communication. With ESA, the favored model for communication between components is asynchronous behavior with forward error recovery. Exceptions to this rule are, of course, allowed and tolerated.

The main exception to the all-synchronous-all-the-time approach applies to user interfaces. Here, a user requests or changes information directly, and this obviously requires a synchronous response. Other examples would include requesting a pre-note or checking a credit limit. Actions like these cannot be completed until an answer is received; you wouldn't want to release funds for withdrawal without knowing whether a credit limit had been exceeded.

5.6 Service Providers and Consumers

Classes of providers

Within the universe of consumers and providers, there is considerable diversity, especially with regard to the different classes of providers. A primary dichotomy exists between providers that host business objects and those that do not. Examples of the latter category would be services that do calculations—pricing engines, interest calculators, balance reconcilers, and so forth—without being in charge of a specific business object. (A business object is an identifiable business entity such as a customer, a contract, or a product that is defined once and becomes a building block of the business. It is described by a data model, an internal process model, and one or more service interfaces.)

Services that host business objects face a rather interesting but devilish challenge: How many instances of a given business object do, or should exist, within the enterprise or even within the value chain? In theory, a business object should have only one instance. (Why allow any confusion or irregularity to exist for something of such importance to the enterprise?) In the real world, however, IT resources tend to be deployed across several instances or multiple computing centers. It is especially true for larger banks and insurers that a customer account might reside in one system, account management functionality in another, and loan management in a third.

Instances of business objects

Some business objects tend to be accessed frequently, a prominent example being a party or business partner. Many processes require access to party information, and there's also a frequent need to change it. In a distributed landscape, access is achieved by providing remote access to instances of the party's business object. In a more unified landscape, enterprises tend to rely on some form of business object redundancy. This turns out to be a double-edged sword. Redundancy is a well-known benchmark for improving performance, but it also creates significant challenges when you try to synchronize or replicate changes across many instances of a business object.

If redundancy is the preferred mechanism for handling multiple instances of a business object, and when a change is made to a single instance, you must ensure that the alteration is distributed outwards in a consistent direction. On the surface, synchronization (or bidirectional updating) appears to be a desirable approach; however, it's virtually unmanageable in a distributed landscape. Here, redundancy is tricky but manageable. Finally, even though there are some business objects that don't suffer too badly in a multiple instance environment ("party," "issuer," etc.), there are others for which having more than one instance is downright unthinkable. This sacrosanct collection includes business objects like "contract," "account," "balance," and other key entities for which there can be only one version of the truth at a given point in time.

Managing redundancy

The situation is more relaxed with providers that don't host a business object. As long as a service is governed by a contract, there can be many other providers that do more or less the same task, even with different implementations. It's also a simple matter to exchange one provider for another, or to have several different providers tackling the same task concurrently.

> **Conclusion:** ESA helps maintain clear distinctions about the separation of concerns that should exist between service providers and service consumers. In addition to drawing borders based on a business perspective, ESA also addresses issues such as reducing or preventing redundancy in order to create highly productive IT environments.

5.7 Service Implementation

Services—and their contracts—are independent of their implementation. Moreover, any service can have more than one implementation. This flexibility holds true even when there can be only one valid implementation linked to a service; for example, when handling a specific customer's account. However, even though services are, or should be, independent from implementation, there are still some service properties that are specific to the implementation. One such example is the semantic contract, which we discussed earlier in this chapter. In addition, there are several non-functional contracts that also link specifically to implementation. These non-functional contracts pertain to attributes, such as a service's performance, borders, capacity, and the conditions before and after a service's invocation. Technical contracts like these tend to be defined during configuration and implementation, and not during modeling time.

Security and performance

Without question, the non-semantic properties that get the most attention in an IT environment are security and performance. Can a service meet the high-pressure demands of a consumer for both volume and response? Setting aside the performance issue for just a moment, the following criteria are also important when considering service implementation:

▶ Does a service provide the security required by all possible consumers? From a security perspective, there may be times when a specific service should *not* be offered to all consumers. It might, for example, be a bad idea to provide employee information over the Internet.

▶ Does a service comply with current regulatory requirements? This question triggers a discussion of version management issues.

- ▶ Which version of a service is currently being used, and is there—or should there be—a newer version?

- ▶ What is the cost for use of the service, and is there a cheaper alternative?

From a technical implementation point of view, SAP sees the use of Web services based on commonly accepted standards as the core tactic for implementing ESA. Many other members of the software community agree with this perception, which is questioned only occasionally within two specific implementation scenarios. First, as noted above, there is some concern that Web services aren't quite muscular enough to sustain high-performance functionality. And secondly, some observers worry that Web services may not fully support critical areas where a high quality of services is required. Examples would include ensuring that a payment is booked only once and that the ordering of messaging is observed.

Accepted standards

One way to sustain a high quality of services is to use the latest standards for reliable messaging; these new norms are proving to be highly effective and pragmatic. The performance issue, however, is still something of a challenge. For financial services companies, performance is critical for many key processes (payments, in particular) and Web services, along with related technologies and protocols, are not considered robust enough to provide the necessary speed and power. That said, there are a number of ways in which Web services can close the performance gap:

- ▶ The performance of Web services can be enhanced by several techniques, including binary protocols and fast parsers.

- ▶ Compared to some existing protocols (such as remote function call in SAP or remote method invocation in Java), Web services can be slower by a factor of two. In most cases, however, this is detrimental only if the time spent parsing or generating messages and serialization or de-serialization makes up a significant part of the overall response time. If most of the time is spent within the application, the Web services overhead can be ignored.

- ▶ Exceptions prove the rule. If a process *must* be supported by something other than a Web service, so be it. As long as exceptions are well documented and well known, this departure from the norm is fully justified.

- ▶ Serious performance issues associated with a specific service may be caused by borders not having been set appropriately. On the other hand, even with judiciously drawn borders, there may be some high-volume areas that demand the highest performance possible.

Conclusion: While there are still some open issues, and some solutions remain under construction, one of the main advantages of enterprise services over pure Web services is that they use standardized semantics. This results in reduced conversion efforts and lower IT costs.

5.8 Deployment

In this chapter, we've talked a lot about the interchangeability of consumers and providers in an ESA environment. A provider can easily exchange one implementation for another, as long as the replacement adheres to the associated contract. The same holds true for consumers. We've also discussed the concept of granularity, especially with regard to providers; with higher granularity comes more freedom to choose other implementations.

Remember, however, that because many different services may depend on the same business object, granularity is not defined within the service itself but at the software component level. Since, as a result of MDA, software components are closely mapped to business objects, the granularity of a business object is mirrored in the linked components. Let's look at an example: a current account, which has to keep track of movements (such as payments), and the actual balances on accounts. Even if movements and balances are distinct business objects with their respective fine-grained services, you wouldn't want to separate them into different software components.

Conclusion: Thanks to flexible deployment options, banks and insurers can leverage ESA-enabled solutions across many different IT landscapes and business structures. By providing the right balance between conflicting needs for both integration and loose coupling, ESA helps financial services firms to prepare for future challenges such as breaking up the value chain, entering new markets, and fending off new competitors.

An IT landscape that helps to achieve goals like these would be hard to resist. So now let's find out how to build one …

6 Designing an Application Landscape with Enterprise Services Architecture

When we think of the term "design" in the context of architecture, we often picture a model of some kind. For building architects like Ludwig Mies van der Rohe or Frank Lloyd Wright, the model would be a blueprint or sketch, that is, a rendering of what a house or other building will look like after it is built. In reality, however, the development of a model is the second step in the design process; it is an outcome of conceptual thinking and certain design processes that govern the way architecture is developed. In this chapter, we'll look at enterprise services architecture design from both perspectives: the design process and the architectural plan (including its main building blocks, enterprise services).

6.1 A Top-Down Approach That Means (and Starts with) Business

For financial services companies, realizing something as substantial as a services-based IT architecture can be achieved only by dividing the work into manageable portions—the various development projects that comprise dedicated design and implementation phases. These projects normally run simultaneously and somewhat independently of each other, so it's important to ensure that they adhere to the common underlying structures and guidelines of the overall architectural model. This, of course, is a management challenge; it demands that you spend a fair amount of time contemplating how to organize service-oriented architecture (SOA) design work from both a procedural and organizational perspective.

Another important point to keep in mind about enterprise services architecture is that although ESA is driven by many new models and precepts, its foundations are built on proven, well-tested principles of design and development. In a sense, the ESA design approach encompasses what has collectively evolved as IT best practices over the last 3 decades.

Still, ESA goes beyond the aggregate total of best practices to date. The main difference lies with the introduction of enterprise services. As amalgamations of Web services that possess enterprise-level business value, enterprise services add another dimension to IT landscapes—a dimension that opens the door to applications with profoundly enhanced business value. From a design standpoint, this means starting with the business context and then developing a roadmap that leads to the generation of business value. That's why ESA design is often referred to as business-driven solution design.

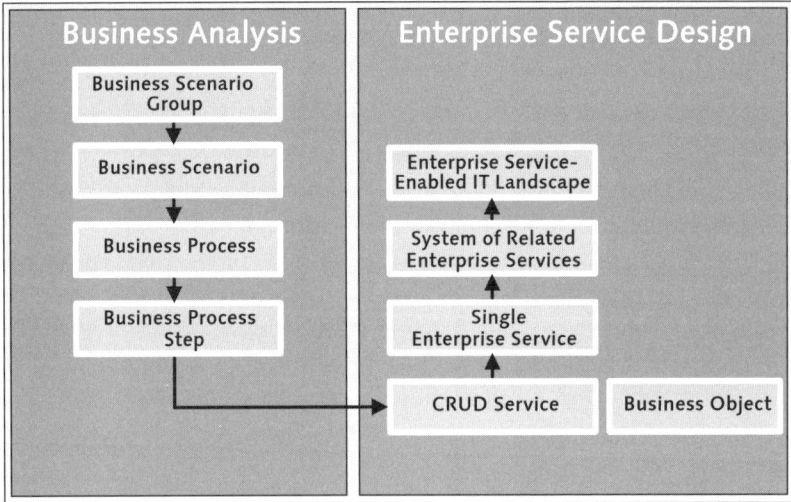

Figure 6.1 The ESA Design Approach

As can be seen in Figure 6.1, business scenarios come first, then processes, then process steps. Once these are completely understood, they are transformed into value-adding services, which are then composed of applications and services-based IT landscape components. This flow is, in essence, the primary concept we'll be exploring in this chapter.

6.2 Business-Driven Solution Design

Steps in solution design

Solution design can be understood as all the activities that go into devising and creating an IT solution. Although there are different approaches to solution design, they all tend to be based on the following steps:

▶ **Identify a problem at the business level**
While the actual problem has a way of making itself known—sometimes quite forcefully—it is also important to make sure that one understands the business processes related to the problem and then to identify requirements for a solution.

▶ **Develop an idea to solve the problem**
This might be an entire IT landscape, an application, a component, or a feature needed to meet certain requirements.

▶ **Evaluate and improve the idea and related business processes**
This step should be undertaken by all interested parties inside and, if necessary, outside the organization.

▶ **Revise the idea and the related processes as needed**
The goal here is to ease implementation by using the existing components and by having discussions with the engineers who will build the solution.

▶ **Describe the idea comprehensively and unequivocally**
A clear depiction makes the idea easier to implement and communicate to all interested parties.

▶ **Implement the idea**

Usually these steps are triggered when an insurance company or bank finds that it has a substantial problem area or pain point. This happens, for example, when an existing IT solution cannot support the business processes needed to develop new offerings, enter new markets, or create the profitability demanded by shareholders. Once identified, this discomfort then results in the creation of a requirements document. Next, the design process is usually initiated at various levels, depending on the problem at hand and the needs of the organization. At a mid-sized or small company, a business analyst may combine the outcome of the steps listed above into a single document. This, in turn, is reviewed by users and IT staff, who then implement the solution in a highly collaborative fashion, with lots of informal communication and adjustment. At a large company, the various steps tend to be assigned to different groups of people, with a more formal methodology applied at each stage, along with various governance and review processes.

The introduction of enterprise services to this flow does not change the design process fundamentally. However, it does add a dimension that supports a new way of building applications, which deliver substantial business benefits. In addition to the use case, user interface, business process, and data flow descriptions, ESA solution design also involves determining what enterprise services should be built as part of a solution, and how these services work together to support business processes.

A new dimension

Enterprise services can be developed by many players throughout the financial services community—by SAP, of course, but also by other business software vendors, by partners, and by banks and insurers. As this book is being written, many enterprise services already exist. This is a highly encouraging state of affairs; as more and more enterprise services become available, the need to reinvent the wheel diminishes. With a large basket of prebuilt elements at one's disposal, building or enhancing a solution becomes a matter of deciding how to use existing services in order to achieve a desired result, rather than building new solutions from scratch. The result is that as financial services companies deploy enterprise services within their solution landscapes, they gain the power to quickly assemble and reassemble applications using services from all the different systems they have in their IT portfolio, thereby enhancing their flexibility.

Why enterprises adopt ESA Here's how enterprise services help to achieve this goal:

▶ **The implementation of an enterprise service is unusually flexible**
Because enterprise services are essentially a definition of an interface and the behavior that each operation should have, they can be implemented by a functional business component, an enterprise application, or custom development.

▶ **Enterprise services allow clear segmentation of a problem area** This enables architects to better control complexity and steer clear of tightly coupled, brittle interaction between different pieces of a solution. Services can be orchestrated so that they reflect the process flow of the end-to-end business processes they support.

▶ **Enterprise services promote tight mapping of business solutions to business realities**
Enterprise services have much finer granularity than traditional IT packages. In other words, instead of being forced to deploy a complete IT solution, enterprise services support deployment of any required functionality in a clearly defined and sharply focused context. In many cases, the service components at hand can be configured to meet business needs. In other situations, a new service component may have to be modeled and implemented. Generally, the granularity of service components at the business level provides a much tighter fit to business requirements compared with full-fledged solutions.

▶ **Enterprise services allow easy orchestration**
With ESA, the service invocation order can easily be rearranged as needed. This means that template business rules, delivered with a standard solution, can be reconfigured so that different paths can be followed through the process model, depending on the available business requirements. This helps to avoid or reduce the development effort necessary to adapt conventional IT environments to specific business needs.

6.2.1 Speaking the Language of Business

Many people assume that enterprise service design is a technical task, akin to designing application programming interfaces (APIs). This notion stems from the fact that Web services tend to perform highly technical functions. Designing enterprise services, however, is not technical but an extension of business process analysis. Because of their inherent emphasis on semantics (see Chapter 5), enterprise services are closely linked to business functions, and can be said to serve as the "language of business."

ESA design as a business task

Easy to say, hard to do. In order for IT to really speak the language of business, there must be a common understanding between business and IT people alike. To learn how the business-driven approach can work, let's look at what SAP does to determine the needs of financial services companies and incorporate those needs into enterprise services and business software.

At SAP, the solution designer's first priority is to be thoroughly knowledgeable about industry business requirements and application areas. The designer must also have a clear understanding of how well SAP solutions support processes with existing functionality, while concurrently seeking to discover new functionality that might be needed. As a first step in determining how applications will meet industry needs, solution designers use a tool called a "solution map" to record the key business scenarios, business processes, and process steps. Solution maps are, to be sure, SAP-centric, but they're a good example of how to structure business requirements using a top-down approach to identify where there are gaps which need to be filled to meet business requirements.

Solution maps

The solution map in Figure 6.2 shows how this business-focused approach can work in an insurance environment. The analysis starts with the highest-level business scenario groups, and then focuses more sharply downward through business scenarios and processes, until it finally drills down to single process steps such as the treatment of a Notice-of-Loss in our example.

Business-focused drill down

Note that the business issues come first, IT activities second; one does not even begin to consider the use of enterprise services or service components until the business scenario has been fully evaluated and understood.

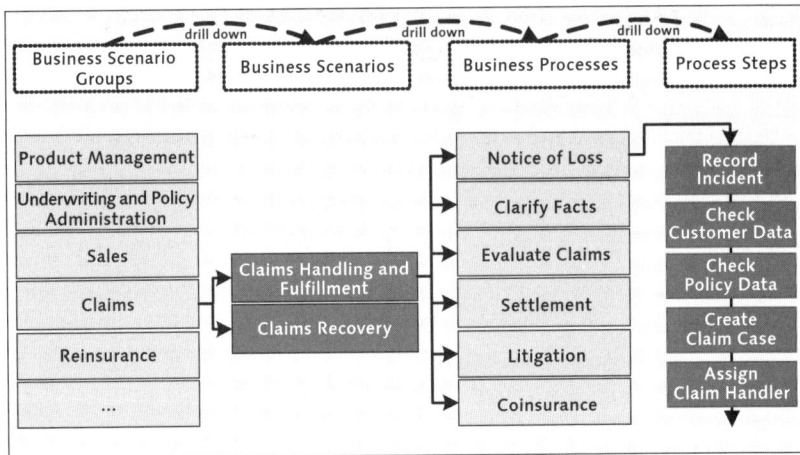

Figure 6.2 Example of a Business Scenario: Insurance—Notice of Loss

In some cases, an existing solution—from SAP, from a third-party provider, or from an insurance company or bank—will provide a perfect fit with business requirements. This is often the case with traditional business processes that have become well understood over time. However, it's far more likely—especially with processes that are evolving to meet new demands—that there will be a functionality gap between existing solutions and user requirements.

Bridging functionality gaps

One way to eliminate the functionality gap would be to build a solution that meets a larger scope of needs. This approach works to a certain extent; however, the danger is that the overall effectiveness of the solution will be hampered. This is because solutions create the most value when they meet common requirements associated with similar tasks or activities within companies (or within industries). Yet, if one tries to make a solution do too many different things, it tends to become agonizingly complex and loses its effectiveness.

With ESA, the functionality gap is closed by deploying enterprise services, which provide the missing functionality as new requirements are identified. Because enterprise services can be called easily by any consumer, and since they use common semantics and ingrained business logic, they amount to "building blocks on demand." Assuming they've been designed correctly, these building blocks will be big enough to support business processes efficiently, and not so small that the job of recombining them becomes aggravating.

6.3 A Step-by-Step Approach to Designing Enterprise Services

How, exactly, do enterprise services help fill the gaps in the IT landscapes of financial services companies? One key to answering this question is to recognize that enterprise services come in different flavors and shapes. Similarly, the IT landscapes of financial services enterprises tend to be quite complex and they, too, have different issues and characteristics at different levels of the environment. In Chapter 5, we introduced the concept of defining services in terms of their granularity and their applicability within either an A2A or B2B landscape. Let's now revisit and expand on this topic to gain a better understanding of the different types of enterprise services and the roles they play within an IT environment.

Types of enterprise services

▶ **Single enterprise services**
tend to be the first step into the world of ESA, but they can nevertheless enhance productivity and power a number of business processes.

▶ **Systems of related enterprise services**
work together to meet more complex requirements such as supporting operational processes associated with key activities like account management, contract administration, or service fulfillment.

▶ **Enterprise services across an IT landscape**
introduce enterprise services into the largest possible number of applications. On this level, questions arise concerning pattern building, reuse, the need to address lifecycle management issues, and other landscape-level issues.

As one might expect, these three levels build on each other. Level two and level three can't be realized unless the levels below are in place. In addition, each of the three levels addresses a different challenge; sometimes an analysis of business processes may reveal that a single service will be all that is needed; at other times, a system of services will be required. The most ambitious level is obviously the structuring of entire IT landscapes, where the design challenge is to improve the ability of many different applications to serve business needs by creating and deploying enterprise services.

6.3.1 Single Enterprise Service

A single enterprise service can be a powerful tool for meeting various goals. For example, a service can collect information that is spread across many systems and present it in a consolidated format in a single screen, thereby boosting user productivity. Automated tasks like these represent opportunities for most financial services companies if achievable short-term. So, in order to get a better understanding of how single services provide value, let's examine how and where their functionality comes into play by looking at the four primary categories of an enterprise service:

▶ Component Services

▶ Process Services

▶ Entity/engine Services

▶ Utility Services

Component Services

A component service monitors relationships that cannot be represented by a data field. It tracks the context, that is, the relationships, data and external information, associated with a business function. A good example would be a credit management service—something that provides information about a customer's credit limit and existing account balances. Additionally, the component service might also manage access to credit ratings, current outstanding payments, and payment history. Such information could be provided by other services consumed by the credit management service.

This leads us to an important distinction about services. When—as described above—a service consumes other services in order to provide a result, we call it a *compound service*. Enterprise services are almost invariably compound services because they tend to include a high level of business context; the business requirements they meet are somewhat complex and cannot be fulfilled at the most granular level. But, there are services that access a single business object or single supporting function. These services cannot be further reduced and they are known as CRUD (Create, Retrieve, Update, and Delete) services.

Process Services

A process service triggers and manages the execution of a process or a process step. When invoked, a process service almost always controls execution by orchestrating other services or other functionality, as needed, to get the job done. Take closed-loop request processing, for example; as a financial services company receives electronic payment requests from customers, it uses the data and functionality of back-office applications to respond to these requests automatically, whenever possible. In some cases, however, an automatic response cannot be generated and a manual workflow must be triggered. To address all possible outcomes, a closed-loop processing service must have a service level that guarantees that the request will either be processed automatically or via human intervention. A service capable of managing both alternatives is quite different from a service that guarantees only that an instruction will be successfully received. In either case, the interface may be identical, but the underlying functionality of the closed-loop request processing service is more powerful.

Entity Services and Engine Services

As their names imply, entity services provide access to the data of an entity—typically a business object—while engine services provide similar functionality with respect to engines like rate calculators or price calculators. Typical tasks of an entity service are to ensure that a business object is properly created according to rules for data completeness and validation. The following examples illustrate the design specifics of these services:

▶ Payment order as an entity service

An entity service that supports payment orders may offer some basic core services to create, retrieve, update, or delete an order. It should also offer services for specific functions that are commonly used in business processes (for example, changing the value date of a payment).

▶ Rating engine service

A service-powered rating engine may provide rate calculations based on a set of input data, as well as all services necessary to maintain rating conditions. An example would be a service that provides quotes for life insurance or property/casualty products.

Utility Services

Utility services provide commonly used functionality for other services or for consumers of services. Although they're not closely linked to business objects, utility services are found in almost all applications and come in very handy when one wants to build a user interface or integrate two applications. Examples of utility services include a value help (a drop-down menu that contains a selection of predefined values for a given entry field), or an authorization check which makes sure that only entitled users are allowed to perform a certain task.

6.3.2   How Single Enterprise Services Add Value

Types of business value

Categorizing enterprise services by their functionality is one way of evaluating their potential impact. More importantly, the categories can be used as a context for looking at the business value that enterprise services provide. After participating in numerous design cycles with its customers, SAP has identified four main areas of improvement:

▶ User productivity and ease of use

▶ Support for process innovation

▶ Business automation and process efficiency

▶ Deployment flexibility

In the next sections of this chapter, we'll take a closer look at each of these benefits.

6.3.3   User Productivity and Ease of Use

User interaction

Enterprise services make it relatively easy to build task-specific user interfaces. Take, for example, an activity that requires users to enter data on ten different screens of the underlying business applications. Now imagine how much more productive the user would be if the ten screens are replaced by just one and a service is introduced that collects the user's entries and distributes them to the appropriate applications. This enhanced ease of use would result in higher efficiency, reduced need for training and, presumably, greater job satisfaction for the user. Customers and partners could also benefit from streamlined user interfaces, because they could enter or obtain information directly instead of using fax, phone, or Electronic Data Interchange (EDI) to send or receive data. In addition, services can help create custom-tailored interfaces to support specific needs and job functions.

Remember, however, that enterprise services don't actually create new user interfaces; they *allow* them to be created. Thanks to the separation of user interface components from business logic, a single service (or single set of services) can enable many different users to have their own role-related screens. This decoupling allows substantial reuse of business logic, and this potential for recycling is one of the most significant characteristics of ESA. Reuse of business logic makes it easy and cost-effective to implement many task-specific and role-specific interfaces. Without the decoupling of components and business logic, one would be sorely tempted to reduce the number of user interfaces in order to keep implementation and maintenance under control. This, in turn, would have a negative effect on productivity and user acceptance.

6.3.4 Next Business Practices and Process Innovation

In addition to custom-tailored user environments, enterprise services support a wide range of new and innovative business processes that would otherwise be difficult to manage. These innovations are sometimes called "next practices" because, if successful, they are likely to be imitated and become best industry practices. Examples of recent next practices are electronic customer channels such as direct banking, and online insurance offerings. Before these services existed, customers had to visit branches or make phone calls to be sure their needs and requests would be met. This process often took hours or even days. Now, thanks to available-to-promise enterprise services that can access important details in back-office applications or data marts, banks and insurers can answer customer queries and commit to fulfilling an order while the customer is still online. Not only does this result in happier customers and more efficient service reps, it also increases cross-sell opportunities.

"Next practices"

Enterprise services that develop next practices frequently find that they can bring IT into precise alignment with business needs. Existing processes, supported by an application, remain in place, while services built on top of the applications allow for enhancements.

6.3.5 Business Automation and Process Efficiency

Another significant virtue of enterprise services is that they frequently enable the complete automation of a task that has been only partially automated in the past. Services also allow IT architects and solution designers to automate particularly annoying or inefficient activities like control and authorization or document provisioning. In addition, services can even provide missing functionality, or solve an integration problem that has not yet been addressed.

Complete task automation

An example of a service that enhances business process automation and efficiency would be "no-touch" claims handling. Today, when a new case arrives in an insurance carrier's environment, someone may have to record the case manually; then, someone else checks to confirm that the claim does not yet exist in the system; and then, a third person might

Example: claims handling

have to take all the documents created up to this point in order to do a fraud detection check. This process typically takes several days. With ESA, however, there may be a no-touch claims-handling service that checks important details in customer and policy administration systems, does an automated fraud check, records all results, and finally initiates the automated clearing process. This drives down response times to a fraction of the previous manual process. Furthermore, if an insurer requires additional processing steps, it is relatively easy to expand the scenario. This versatility enables carriers to respond to customer notices quickly and efficiently, while maintaining a very high level of data consistency.

Continuing this gratifying scenario, the no-touch claims-handling service could also help to automate data entry by providing an interface to a scanner or an electronically-transmitted XML notice, check the data, then enter the notice in a system. If desired, the service could also check whether all information needed to respond to the claim is available and, if so, automatically complete the claim. Moving far beyond its humble Web services origin, business-driven enterprise services, like the one we've just posited, can make a substantial contribution to key business goals such as cutting costs, increasing efficiency, and improving customer service.

6.3.6 Deployment Flexibility

Flexible deployment options

Enterprise services that enable flexible deployment options increase the choices available to those who manage applications. This results in a number of potential benefits. Take the process of submitting an account statement; services can be used to redirect the flow of these documents without any change in the way the reports are submitted. They could be directed straight to a customer, to a clerk who might need to perform a manual processing step, to someone in a central office who would use an automated system to process the report, or even to one or more third-party processing firms.

6.3.7 Business Benefits and Functional Categories

Benefit/function correlation

In a sense, the design of enterprise services is driven by matching functional categories to business benefits. SAP's early experience with enterprise service design has revealed a fairly consistent correlation between business benefits and the functional category of the services needed to realize a business outcome.

Business Benefits / Single Services Categories	User productivity and centricity	Next business practices and process innovation	Business automation and process efficiency	Flexible deployment and platform
Component			■	■
Process		■	■	■
Entity/Engine	■	■	■	■
Utility	■	■		■

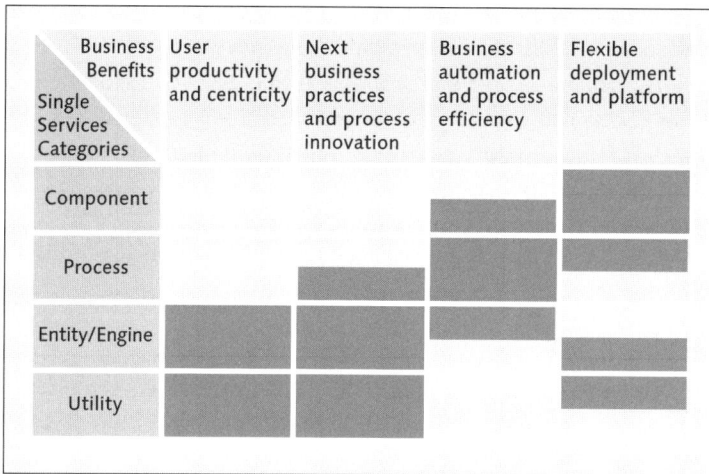

Figure 6.3 Functional Service Categories and Business Benefits

Functional categories

As shown in Figure 6.3, the benefit/function matrix can help architects visualize, evaluate, and fine-tune design ideas. Here's how the various services map to four key functional categories and how they help generate business benefits:

▶ **User productivity**

tends to increase when customized user interfaces are deployed. Interface elements like a work center or interactive form tend to be supported by entity/engine services, along with corresponding utility services. Process services are less important, because the user is driving the process.

▶ **Process innovation**

is typically supported by composite applications. Just as with GUIs, a user controls the process; this means that entity/engine services and their associated utilities are required. A composite application may also trigger a process, and then hand over control to the next application. In this case, a process service would be required.

▶ **Business automation**

usually includes one application calling another. In this peer-to-peer situation, control is handed over to the called application. This activity falls squarely in the domain of process services.

▶ **Flexible deployment**

focuses on managing the execution of business objects and processes represented by components. In some cases, entity/engine services or utilities may also be required.

It is important to note that the benefits described above—and consequently the scope of the services defined—are not mutually exclusive.
Achieving one business benefit frequently produces a set of requirements
that becomes the source of new processes and the services that support
them. So, there's often a cross-pollination effect that results in more efficient processes, faster response-to-market opportunities, and lower
operating expenses.

6.4 Systems of Related Enterprise Services

Cooperating
enterprise services

In Section 6.3 we discussed the characteristics and benefits associated
with single services. Yet, despite the tangible value that single services
provide, ESA really begins to deliver value through design and management of groups of cooperating enterprise services. In most cases, complex business processes can be supported only by services working
together, and in this section, we'll be discussing ways in which systems of
enterprise services can meet the many needs of banks and insurance
companies.

An Example for Systems of Related Enterprise Services: The FNOL Scenario

What are systems of related services? As an example, let's use first
notice of loss (FNOL) from the insurance industry. We'll assume that
an automobile has incurred damage and that the owner has contacted
the carrier to claim that the damage be covered under an existing
insurance policy. This request triggers a claims process at the insurer.
Almost invariably, the directive to post an FNOL document triggers
many other cross-functional and cross-application activities. These
activities would include sending a confirmation to the claimant, post-
ing the FNOL document to the claims registry, checking that the claimant is known in the customer information file, performing an initial
coverage check, running a fraud inquiry, notifying the responsible customer contact, and assigning an employee in another department to
act as the claims handler.

Today, this scenario tends to be managed somewhat inefficiently; the processes depend on a fair amount of manual work and there are usually workflow disruptions that stem from integration gaps in existing IT solutions. The antidote? Turn the claims process into an available-to-promise (ATP) service, supported by an ecosystem of enterprise services all working together. An ATP service for the claims process would be implemented using services that query several internal systems across multiple instances, as well as services provided by partners. This collaboratively interlocked system of services might also include those that invoke a car rental or towing request, order an appraiser, or locate a garage to take care of the damage. Claims processing managers could also use services from suppliers or logistics partners that are several levels removed from the policy writing insurance company.

In addition to claims management, systems of enterprise services are capable of supporting a great many activities and processes. However, the inherent dependence on cooperation means that systems of services have characteristics that don't apply to single services. These characteristics, which might be areas of concern, are:

Areas of concern

▶ Informal support for business transactions

▶ Support for analytics and accounting

▶ Management of master data

▶ Maintaining relationships between business objects under the ownership of different functional components

6.4.1 Business Transaction Support

Most business processes are designed to handle mistakes, errors and cancellations rather elegantly. So are most of the IT solutions that support the processes. From the database level up, the term "transaction support" describes the ability to initiate a process, but then roll back the work if something goes wrong. At the database level, this includes opening a transaction, taking a snapshot, or creating a checkpoint that preserves the current state, doing the required work, and finally either committing the transaction (making the changes permanent) or aborting the transaction and rolling back the changes to the checkpoint.

Error handling

When business transactions span long periods of time—days, weeks, or even months—transactional support on the database level alone is not sufficient. Instead, the tendency is to rely on a transaction monitor, especially in a distributed environment. The monitor keeps track of transactions in all related systems and then commits or rolls back the changes in each of the systems as needed. There are times, however, when financial services business processes—and their related IT solutions—face circumstances that are even more complex. For example, sometimes one may need to undo operations that are aborted during the execution of a business process. This task is similar to transactional support, but somewhat fuzzier, which is why it's often referred to as "informal" transaction support.

Services for transaction support

ESA handles informal transaction support rather deftly through the use of enterprise services. Where a given process needs transactional support of some kind, service operations are created that express this functionality at a high level. (A service operation is executable functionality that is described in the interface to a service.) Typically, a number of services are used; one service operation expresses the beginning of the transaction, while other service operations can express committing or rolling back. Sometimes rolling back is the only service that needs to be exposed, because opening and committing the transaction happen as part of the normal process. Note that these service operations need not be implemented with commit and rollback functions on a database level. Instead, they can do and undo work in order to restore changed data to its original state. At the same time, they may also record whatever has almost happened should this be necessary for meeting auditing requirements.

6.4.2 Support for Analytics and Accounting

Analytics, accounting and reporting requirements

From a business perspective, accounting, analytics, and reporting are cornerstones of daily work. From a solution design standpoint, however, they are often ignored. One of the main reasons for this oversight is that since data collection is laborious, it's frequently postponed until later phases of development projects. This means that many enterprises define their analytics design *after* defining their operational data structures. Regrettably, this procrastination can result in high costs; operational systems frequently have to be upgraded or enhanced to meet new accounting, analytical, and reporting requirements.

For example, many operational systems are set up to accommodate local accounting standards. However, this local orientation becomes a problem when a bank or insurer wants to enter non-domestic markets or gain access to international capital. In these cases, international accounting standards must also be observed. This leaves the enterprise with two choices: adapt current systems to the new rules (understanding that this will have to be done again and again whenever the rules change over time), or redesign the responsibilities of the accounting and valuation services, stripping them away from the operational systems. The latter choice makes a great deal of sense, especially because regulators seem to be demanding that accounting and analytical information should be reported together and reported consistently. From an IT perspective (shared by SAP and a number of banks, insurers, and other software providers), there seems to be clear agreement that in order to ensure future flexibility and adaptability, accounting and regulatory requirements need to be separated from operational applications. One of ESA's most significant virtues is its ability to create a landscape in which this decoupling can be accomplished more easily.

Another issue arises from the huge volumes of data extracted from operational systems for analytical purposes. Although this may happen at only certain times, the IT infrastructure must be able to deal with the occasional peaks. Finally, extraction from operational sources is an "ex-post" concept—one that works against a base of historic data. Along with the peak volume issue, this often leads to situations where users are presented with stale or obsolete information.

Data volume peaks

Systems of enterprise services are very helpful for addressing the aforementioned issues. ESA-based systems anticipate the need to assemble data for analytical and reporting usage by creating sets of related services (including an analytics and monitoring service), which allow all the other services to send data. This cluster of analytic enterprise services takes care of consolidating and storing the data at the point in time when it first emerges. The structure may also utilize information-hiding and loose coupling in order to reduce data loads at peak times. All in all, system and process management capabilities like these help enterprise services architecture generate substantial value for IT landscapes and the business processes they support.

Cluster of analytic enterprise services

6.4.3 Management of Master Data

In the previous chapter, we discussed ESA's role in the definition and management of frequently accessed business objects. Most financial services companies make changes to these objects quite often. Since many business processes and their related IT solutions depend on these business objects and require access to them, they are often referred to as master data—prominent examples of which are a party, customer, or

Master data in distributed and unified landscapes

business partner. In distributed landscapes, systems of related services that handle central master data can be an effective means of providing remote access to instances of these objects. In more unified landscapes, where enterprises tend to rely on some form of business object redundancy, systems of related distribution services may be used to replicate changes across instances of business objects to the related IT solutions, using controlled redundancy as a way to improve system performance.

6.4.4 Relationships

Relationships between business objects

Managing relationships between business objects is another issue that often arises in IT landscapes characterized by application silos. For example, many financial services companies maintain a file with core information on customers. The file is typically accessed by applications that support different lines of business: one for current customer accounts, one for financing products, a third for managing pension funds. The responsibility for managing relationships is usually contained in the operational solutions that own the primary business objects. In our example, the account administration system would own the accounts, but would also own the relationship between an account and an account holder; the loan administration system would own the loan and the relationship of the loan to the borrower; and, finally, the pension system would be responsible for the pension contract, but also its relation to the beneficiary and other related parties.

Composite applications

In complex environments (especially when solutions are distributed across multiple instances) systems of services are extremely useful for maintaining relationships between the business objects that are owned by the different components. ESA supports the deployment of composite applications—built on top of the aforementioned applications—that communicate with these solutions through a set of services. Any change of a customer's master data could be entered through the composite, which would distribute the data via services to the customer information file (CIF). The composite would also be able to retrieve the relationship information via corresponding services from the other operational solutions.

6.5 Enterprise Services in the Context of IT Landscapes

Functional business components

Let's assume that a bank or insurance company has put a toe in the service-dappled waters. The first enterprise services have been implemented, tested, and proven successful. Our sample organization has also mastered the challenge of making many services work together. Now, however, the number of available services is rising, perhaps at an alarming rate. How can the service environment remain transparent and supportable? Should one try to manage an almost infinite number of fine-grained "mini" services, which can be snapped together like so many toy blocks? Or should one prebuild groups of services so business applications can be made of preassembled components?

This complexity issue must be solved in order to realize ESA's potential for flexibility, efficiency and cost-reduction. Fortunately, an answer is at hand in the form of an ESA design element known as the *functional business component*, which helps IT architects group related services together, thereby reducing complexity.

Functional Component Example: Credit Management

Let's use a business scenario to illustrate the concept of functional business components. Banks and insurance companies rely on many different functions to handle requests related to credit management. Two examples are a query on whether a credit limit has been exceeded and a request to expand a credit limit. In an ESA environment, these requests can be addressed by service operations, which we'll call *ApproveCreditLimitAvailable* and *ExpandCreditLimit*. Since both services depend on information about a customer's credit limit, it makes sense to implement them as service operations of an enterprise service we'll call *CreditLimitMonitoring*. Managing credit limits, however, usually involves more functions than mere monitoring and, as one might expect, these functions can also be adroitly supported by enterprise services. What's needed, however, is a kind of mastermind—an overseer who can coordinate and integrate everything that goes on within these groups of groups. That's why the ESA design method includes an additional layer that comprises all services related to scenarios or processes such as (in this case) credit management functionality. The additional layer will most likely need a functional component so, to bring our example to a close, we'll assume that the architects choose to create a functional component called *CreditManagement*.

6.5.1   Services with Brainpower

Bundling sets of cognate enterprise services into functional components helps insurance companies and banks in a number of ways. As noted

Software lifecycle management

above, it helps maintain an overview of all the services that may evolve over time in a given area. Functional components also help manage software lifecycle tasks such as versioning and delivery of patches and fixes. In some ways, functional components behave very much like traditional software components, but there are important differences. Since a functional component is purely a collection of enterprise services, it contains only the building blocks found within these services: business objects, the functionality related to these objects, and the interfaces that expose the functionality to the outside. Functional components, therefore, lack certain elements found in traditional components (such as functionality required to interact with users, context-dependent implementations of integration techniques, and the functionality required to manage interaction with other services outside of the functional component). For functional components, these tasks are handled by other, specialized elements of ESA.

Decoupling
This decoupling is one of the most significant aspects of the ESA model. Not only does it assure that attention will be paid to business-related functionality, but it also promotes independence from activities such as the implementation of user interaction tasks, workflow processing, and information provisioning—mundane chores that can be better performed by dedicated tools. The beneficial result of the decoupling is that the core parts of the software that support business objects and their related services become more stable and require fewer updates. This, naturally, reduces the time and effort needed to maintain them. As a result, IT departments free up resources that can be allocated to areas that support differentiation—like customer service, new product development, and revamped business processes.

6.5.2 Establishing Domains

Functional domains
Once a financial services company has embraced the service-powered vision, it becomes easy to imagine an IT environment with 100 or more functional components and perhaps several thousand enterprise services. Assuming that borders have been drawn properly (see Chapter 5), each service has a different set of functions. Achieving this goal at the IT landscape level can result in significant cost savings, especially if related groups of functional components are grouped appropriately within the ESA landscape. Therefore, let's briefly note how functional components can be grouped into domains, depending on the processes they support.

Key process categories include:

▶ **Management processes** that deal with analysis, controlling, and decision-making support on various enterprise levels

▶ **Sales and service processes** that relate to all customer-facing activities

   These processes are supported by online sales and service centers, plus remote mobile services for agents, brokers, and other intermediaries.

▶ **Operational processes** such as the provisioning of in-force and contract administration processes

   This category includes highly specialized core functional processes, as well as cross-functional processes, both of which serve as a backbone for execution and administration.

▶ **Business support processes** that consist of activities required to run an enterprise, but do not create value by themselves

Based on the understanding of business process categories and variations of enterprise services—and with appropriately grouped domains of functional components and the tools and applications needed to make them work—we can now draw a high-level picture of how to structure an IT landscape in the ESA environment (see Figure 6.4).

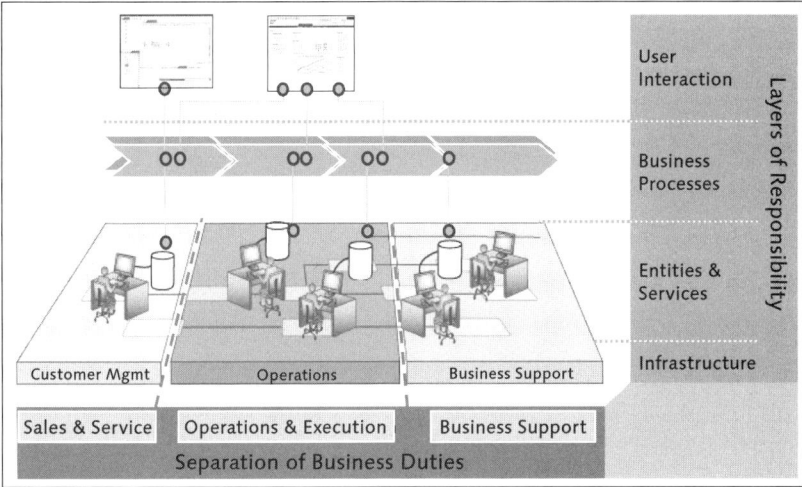

Figure 6.4 Structure of an IT Landscape

6.5.3 Putting Services to Work

Company examples At this point, let's take a short break from the high-level perspective to learn how financial services companies are utilizing SOA and ESA to reach various IT and business goals. Here are four examples of how service-enabling an IT landscape can pay significant dividends:

In the U.S., AAA Carolinas Insurance recently announced that it had achieved a return on its investment in SOA in less than two months, based on reduced policy processing time, lower document handling costs, and a 60 percent spike in customer acquisition and retention. "This architecture gives us the ultimate flexibility," says Harry Johns, the carrier's IT manager. "Where it used to take us weeks to create interfaces, we can now hook products together in a matter of days."[1]

U.S.-based Fireman's Fund Insurance Co. is using SOA to change the way business executives communicate their needs for new products and services to the IT department. "Business models change much more rapidly today," says Fred Matteson, CIO of Fireman's Fund. "Being able to reuse and recombine services into different workflows will bring huge benefits. To me that's the power of it—to finally get a technology representation of how business actually works,"[2] Fireman's Fund, which intends to consolidate 70 percent of its technology applications around an enterprise-wide service-oriented architecture, expects an ROI in excess of $200 million. "And that's just the system's quantified benefits," Matteson notes. "It doesn't start to get into the business value."

Public sector insurers like Germany-based health insurance giant AOK also profit from ESA. As part of the company's effort to modernize its application landscape, AOK is mapping its core business processes to the enterprise services architecture blueprint. The goal is to allow the firm to leverage existing processes (such as setting up new contracts or signing on new policyholders) to create new, combined processes supported by composite applications. AOK anticipates that the software solutions it is currently developing with SAP will help the company lower costs and react more quickly to customer demands and changing legal requirements.

---

1 I&T Staff, Insurance & Technology, *SOA Score*, September 16, 2005, *www.insurancetech.com.*

2 Anthony O'Donell, *Journey to Service-Oriented Architecture*, September 2005, *www.insurancetech.com.*
   Insurance Giant Steps up SAP NetWeaver Footprint for Staff of 60000," SAP Press Release, March 2005.

South Africa-based Standard Bank is using ESA to drive a customer-centric strategy aimed at aligning the bank's services to customer needs over a complete lifecycle, also taking care to offer the services through preferred channels. While Standard Bank currently enjoys a steady 22% growth rate, and its return on earnings and cost of income are far ahead of industry norms, Strategic Programme Manager Jörg Fischer says that the bank wants to solidify customer relationships as international banks push aggressively into the South African market. To meet this challenge, the bank has embarked on a major project to overhaul its core domestic systems. As part of a five-year initiative, Standard Bank will implement what it calls an enterprise architecture framework, starting with the customer master file and ultimately including the underlying transaction systems. Fischer says the decision to start with the Customer Master File was based on the belief that plumbing needed to be in place before solutions could be successfully deployed. "If you start with the product systems," says Fischer, "you end up with the same model as before."[3]

6.5.4 A New Way of Thinking

To be sure, enterprise services architecture design does entail a certain amount of complexity. One must become comfortable with new architectural principles, spend a fair amount of time developing a unified set of semantics, and service-enable current applications and components. Above all, one must learn to focus on business issues at the enterprise level rather than on software issues at the technical level. As we've seen in this chapter, the actual technical skills needed for the ESA design process are relatively straightforward. The challenge is that ESA requires a somewhat different way of thinking about things. The good news here, however, is that since this change of mindset begins with a consideration of fundamental business issues, the resulting decisions and changes flow toward beneficial results: happier customers, reduced costs, a better-focused product portfolio, the ability to recycle resources and innovate almost at will.

The ESA mindset

As we'll see in Chapters 7 and 8, even though the road to ESA will undoubtedly be long, it need not be torturous. Equally important, the journey can produce benefits rather quickly, with a number of quick wins along the way. Because each incremental step tends to generate a payoff, and since the one-step-at-a-time approach allows for coexistence of the

---

3 Standard Bank begins major project. IBS Publishing, June 2005. *http://www.ibs-publishing.com*.

new and the old, each additional ESA investment has a way of justifying itself. In addition, companies like SAP can help fill in potholes and avoid detours. Thanks to its 30-year history of application development and industry expertise, SAP can help speed up the journey with a number of tools and services designed to help banks and insurers put enterprise services to work. In Chapter 7, we'll stress test this assertion by observing what happens as we ESA-enable a current application.

7 Turning ESA into Reality: SAP's Solution Approach

As the principles of service-oriented architecture (SOA) are used to design and build an IT landscape, a number of outcomes ensue. In addition to a useful catalogue of described services, you also get deployable software—a primary goal of any IT department. When it comes to software, enterprise services architecture (ESA) is a blueprint for service-based, enterprise-scale business solutions that offer increased levels of adaptability and flexibility. As such, ESA is all about giving financial institutions freedom of choice, because it allows for easier integration of custom-made applications and vendor solutions. Today, integrating vendor solutions often requires a substantial effort that includes mapping semantic clashes, dealing with overlapping functionality, and sorting out process understanding. ESA helps to reduce these chores to a tolerable level.

As a provider of business software, SAP has a vested interest in making sure that its portfolio of solutions can be easily integrated into its customers' IT environments. To this end, SAP must first make sure that its current solutions can be service-enabled. Then, as new releases become available, SAP must ensure that the latest versions are also equipped to deliver the benefits associated with enterprise services architecture. In this chapter, we'll look at how SAP is managing this transition. Lessons learned will be beneficial not only for current or future SAP customers, but for anyone considering a transition from legacy architecture to a service-enabled environment.

SAP's transition to ESA

7.1 Transforming an Existing Software Application

Having made a decision to tap the power of services, one has two choices when software is concerned: build (or buy) a new ESA-enabled product, or transform an existing application. For now, we'll concentrate on the latter choice, using the transformation of a loan software application as an ongoing example throughout this chapter. Loans have obviously been an important part of the business landscape at banks and insurers for many years, which also means that loan applications have been around for some time. Therefore, it should come as no surprise that most loan applications are more than 10 years old, and that they're characterized by a mix of business functionality, process management, and presentation functionality.

Build, buy or transform?

If a bank or insurer concludes that a loan application should be ESA-enabled, it must be mapped to the target architecture. This process begins with the study and evaluation of two dimensions:

- ▶ Technical layering of an application
- ▶ Business-oriented clustering

7.2 Layering

Presentation, business process, and enterprise services layer

Layering of an application means from a business perspective to distinguish between consumers and providers of enterprise services and to agree on "contracts" (see chapter 5) between them. This thinking leads to technical layering. Technical layering is a matter of decomposing the old software application into three layers—the presentation layer, the business process layer, and the enterprise services layer (the latter represents the business functionality). Within the enterprise services layer, it's a good idea to follow existing industry canons for separation of concerns (see chapter 5), when determining the behavior and grouping of services. If common norms are not observed, it's very likely that the transformation will result in proprietary structures; these can be somewhat convenient within the walls of the corporation, but they reduce the opportunities for value chain collaboration and also create a barrier to the potential benefits of outsourcing.

Common industry preferences

Working closely with members of the financial community, SAP is in the fortunate position of being able to recognize and respond to common industry preferences—the result of much discussion and analysis with prospects, customers, and partners. Getting back to our loan application example, one prevalent industry understanding is that a majority of banks and insurers want this solution to be independent from the output management system that handles statements.

This independent-yet-integrated relationship can be achieved relatively easily by using services that provide data, plus services that provide an output of statements. A transformation of this sort creates a great deal of flexibility for financial services companies; they can decide when the event "print statements" will be executed in the overall process, and they can also decide whether it will happen with an SAP or non-SAP application. This simple example illustrates how easy it is to accelerate or restrict on flexibility. Multiply this single instance by hundreds of others, and you can see how the experience of SAP can help customers transform an application by composing sets of services which are most likely to be accepted throughout the financial services industry.

There is no doubt that a great many banks and insurers (and software providers) would benefit if the industry came up with a mutual understanding of which services are most important and how these services should behave. After all, services implicitly define the boundaries and responsibilities of business functions. In support of industry-wide alignment, SAP has established the Industry Value Network (IVN) to define the services needed for the transition to enterprise services architecture. IVN promotes industry alignment at three levels:

The Industry Value Network (IVN)

▶ Strategic discussions with CIOs who meet to promote acceptance and adoption of upcoming changes

▶ The exchange of best practice concepts and other ideas among Chief Architects

▶ Definition and alignment guidelines for work groups and subject matter experts

At this point, however, let's leave the IVN and its important work and return to our loan application example. The process of transforming it into a service-enabled solution will have two phases: design and implementation.

7.3   Service Design

The loan application supports a business scenario that SAP calls financing. The scenario consists of a number of processes—from origination through servicing and refinancing, and on to valuation and accounting, including risk reporting and stress testing. Within each of these processes, flexible process steps are defined. Each process step, in turn, consumes one or more enterprise services.

From business scenarios to identified services

As mentioned above, enterprise services are defined and modelled in accordance with common business standards; hence, they represent the execution of well-defined business tasks. An important fact to note about the realization of the many processes involved in the "financing" scenario is that they are not hard coded. Instead, the processes orchestrate the consumption of services. Thanks to the inherent neutrality and connectability of services, this results in significant flexibility, allowing banks or insurers to design and redesign their processes as often as they like.

7.4 Service Implementation

Benefits by abstraction and decomposition

The implementation of enterprise services depends, in large part, on software providers, each of whom has a unique approach to this activity. The approach used by SAP, and a number of partners and ISVs, focuses on the abstraction and decomposition of business processes. Though this sounds somewhat alarming, it produces significant benefits, because it allows for the alignment of business goals and IT resources. Abstraction and decomposition result in a versatile, flexible implementation of services, because they are not tightly coupled, they can support virtually any business process.

Example: disbursement of mortgage

To illustrate this concept, let's use the disbursement of a mortgage as an example. The overall process includes many steps, such as checking the completeness of documents, validating the recipient and, depending on the type and amount of a given transaction, generating a release-to-pay. Breaking the disbursement process down even further, it's obvious that there will be a step that involves consuming a service that we'll call *InitiateMoneyTransfer*. While this service is an important link in the disbursement process, it would also be useful in many other situations. Assuming that it has been well designed, the *InitiateMoneyTransfer* service can be consumed by process steps supporting a wide range of products like repayment of fixed-term deposits, payment transfers from checking accounts, or disbursement of consumer loans. This "build it once, use it over and over again" approach can yield substantial benefits. Furthermore, in addition to the actual process steps, associated integration efforts and interfaces are also reusable, which makes service-enabling all the more valuable in the long run.

7.5 Process Platform

Process platform layer

The primary goals of transitioning to a new IT architecture are to increase flexibility, reduce complexity, and lower costs. Reaching these objectives depends, in large part, on shrewd implementation and achieving the right level of abstraction and granularity for enterprise services. With ESA, it's important to understand that the implementation of enterprise services will generate a separate decoupled software layer—one that provides business logic to be consumed by business processes and user interfaces. SAP refers to this layer as a *process platform*—a combination of technology infrastructure and the fundamental business functionality provided by a reusable implementation of enterprise services. To address the need for sector-specific deployments, SAP will offer a Business Process Platform for Banking and for Insurance.

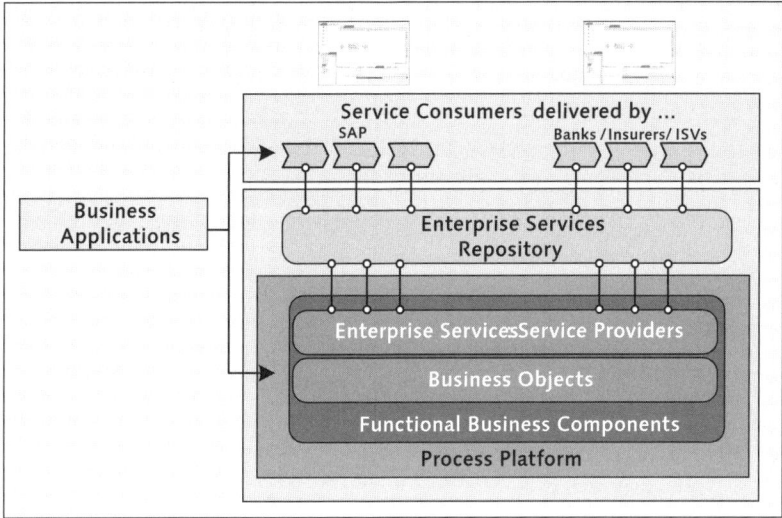

Figure 7.1 SAP's ESA Approach: The Emergence of the Platform Layer

Figure 7.1 shows how the process platform will work within an ESA-powered landscape. SAP's first step has been to sort out the functionality of the various services, delineating their behavior in terms of providers and consumers. This layering of existing applications is an important prerequisite for successful transformation to the ESA target architecture. Mind you, from a business perspective there are consumers (processes and people) who don't really care about the layering of an application. A user interface (UI) would be a good example. The UI does consume services, but it requires a business view—an integrated solution that solves business requirements. Conversely, application layering is an IT activity designed to achieve agility.

Looking at the loan example, this means that all business events in the life cycle of a loan have to be classified into a consumer and a provider perspective. The above example, "disbursement of a mortgage," contains a couple of business events such as "initiate the first, second or last payment". A business event can be executed automatically or with user interaction. Based on this decision the interaction between the UI and the process management tool has to be defined. Both areas belong to the consumer view. Both have to be connected with enterprise services accessing business functionality such as "calculate payment amount" or "post payment."

Layering of applications

7.6 Core Functionality for Financial Services Companies

Process platforms provide a nucleus of core functionality that supports solution deployments within ESA. The platforms are not complete solutions (such as SAP for Banking or SAP for Insurance); instead, they are components that provide ready-to-use enterprise services. It is the solutions themselves which provide the consuming services that support dedicated business processes like loan management, loan valuation, and risk measurement. The process platform serves as a base that helps power many different solutions, whether they're provided by SAP, a partner, a third party or a customer. With the Process Platform, SAP helps customers define and implement new software solutions according to ESA principles.

Process platforms will allow financial services companies to address a multitude of IT and business issues because they are:

▶ **Service based**
enabling process flexibility with well-defined borders

▶ **Built around business object models**
that describe key business semantics and therefore help enterprises speak a common language

▶ **Supported by a well-defined communication paradigm**
for real decoupled integration

With these thoughts in mind, we'll wrap up our discussion of what we referred to as the first of two dimensions at the beginning of this chapter: the technical layering of an existing software application. The layering exercise, repeated as often as needed or desired, results in a transition to required user interfaces, business processes, and enterprise services, which are described in a repository and delivered by custom-made or vendor-sold software. This having been said, it's time to move on to our second dimension, which revolves around the idea of how these enterprise services can be grouped and implemented so that they do the most good.

7.7 Business-Oriented Clustering of Enterprise Services

To gain a better understanding of the process platform, it helps to think of it not as a monolithic layer, but as a provider layer for enterprise services—a kind of universal dispatcher offering access to enterprise services on behalf of any consumer who needs them. The process platform is characterized by reusability; theoretically, every single service can be deployed and offered in a technology-independent environment. But, since services add most value when they are pre-combined in useful patterns, the process platform also contains clusters of services (sometimes called domains)—aggregations of individual services that logically belong together in order to be useful for banks and insurers.

Let's expand our understanding of clusters by looking at a financial transaction such as any kind of payment. It's clear that a process step like creating a payment will be linked to a handful of business objects. These, in turn, will be associated with services which guarantee that payment blocks, payment limits, or other parameters are checked before the payment is initiated. To meet required performance standards, an enterprise service of this type should be implemented in one deployment unit, with all associated services of the business objects in close proximity.

Note, however, that within a cluster, the behavior of the services and the data requirements of the services can be quite different. A consuming service in a sales process—such as one that creates an offer—will expect to capture incomplete data, since the complete data household is not necessary at this stage. This contrasts sharply with the services that are associated with the administration of financial contracts; here, the data must be structured, checked, and monitored by an audit trail. Our sample cluster might also include additional services that help analyze financial instruments and portfolios; these services would have to be capable of performing complex tasks like simulations, stress testing, and creating historical views and future projections.

A cluster need not (and should not) be proprietary. Industry-wide acceptance ultimately allows for the easy substitution or replacement of applications over time—or, more accurately, substitution or replacement of service-providing components. Every financial institution and every software vendor who rallies behind a given cluster can easily restructure existing applications using the predefined boundaries of responsibility.

Proprietarity

7.8 Clusters in the Real World

Let's continue our discussion of clusters by applying the concept to the hypothetical loan application that we've been studying in this chapter. The ESA-enabled loan application has rich functionality all along the value chain, spanning processes like origination, payments, contract monitoring, collection, depreciation and valuation, including local GAAP. Collat-

Example: loan application

eral, too, could be managed with a 1:1 relation to the loan. From a total cost of ownership (TCO) perspective, this would indeed be a comprehensive and beneficial solution. But, imagine how much more valuable the application would be if it could accommodate change in the business environment: new channels with their own, independent origination (e.g., agencies); new combinations of product offerings; changes in regulations like Basel II or accounting principles; the need for independent lifecycles of collaterals; independent optimization of the collection process. ESA accommodates these changes and virtually any other shift in the business ecosystem. As long as the IT landscape is built around independent enterprise services, resources become so modularized that they can be assigned to different service clusters.

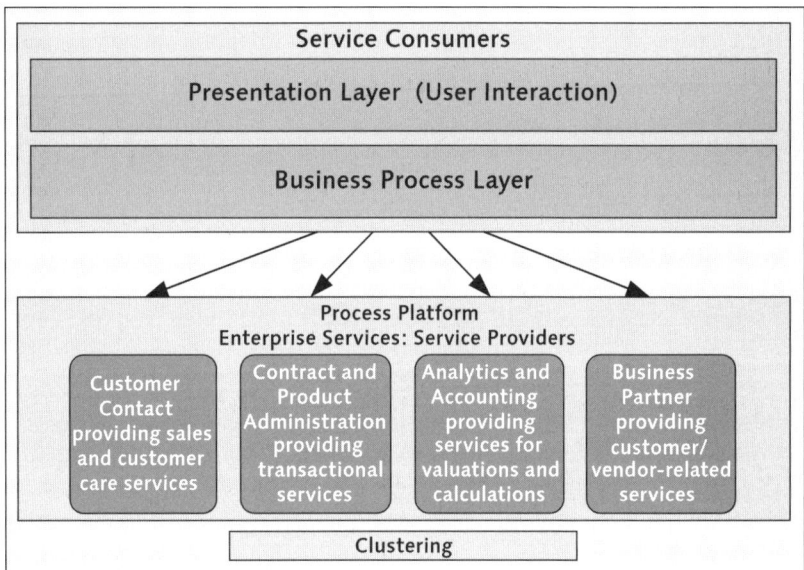

Figure 7.2 Clustering Components According to Areas of Business Responsibilities

Figure 7.2 shows how this apportioning process might sort itself out with respect to our loan application. Following the decomposition principle in the ESA design process, services are assigned to the following clusters:

▶ Origination · Customer Contact (including sales services)

▶ Contract fulfillment, payments, and collection · Contract & Product Administration

▶ Valuation · Analytics & Accounting

▶ Customer data · Business Partner

Because every cluster can be deployed separately, banks and insurers are free to optimize their individual landscapes in the way that fits them best. Contract administration, for example, can be deployed along product lines, including insourced and outsourced options; accounting and regulatory monitoring may be deployed once, acting as a single resource for all financial instruments.

7.9 Technical Perspective

Enterprise services are described in the enterprise services repository (ESR). The process platform provided by SAP is a software layer that manages the central functions of the enterprise's most important business objects. For message management and transaction control, the process platform accesses the infrastructure provided by SAP NetWeaver. Although we've been looking primarily at provider services during our discussion of the process platform, you should note that ESA does not neglect consumer services. SAP NetWeaver provides an infrastructure for the design of user interfaces and business processes. As one might expect, the decoupling of software layers results in a freedom of choice as far as software suppliers are concerned; different products can be used at different places within the stacks. And, getting back to the loan application we've discussed: an ESA-enabled loan solution can be implemented with different technical layers.

Enterprise services repository

7.10 Summing Up the Benefits of the Process Platform

In a financial services environment, SOA is driven by business needs. It requires business and IT leaders to make well informed decisions about how applications should be layered and how services should be clustered. Making these decisions thoroughly will reward banks and insurance companies with software components that provide stable, fine-grained business logic accessible through services. This yields a wide range of benefits:

▶ Accelerated solution offerings
  The process platform provides an environment in which flexible, service-driven solutions can be composed quickly. Whether built by customers (homemade solutions), partners, or SAP, the platform accelerates the creation of best-in-class applications for financial services firms.

► **Flexible deployment scenarios**
The process platform enables customers to design deployment scenarios based specifically on the unique characteristics of their overall system landscape. This reduces TCO and fosters process harmonization.

► **Unified environment for the financial services ecosystem**
Partners will be able to provide solutions for the process platform without increasing integration complexity for banking and insurance customers.

7.11   ESA Ecosystem

Software vendors In addition to supporting standardization activities in the financial services industry, SAP is promoting adoption of ESA by software vendors in other important vertical markets. Intel, Cisco, Microsoft, and others have agreed to support ESA in their products and are certifying a wide variety of products to work in an ESA-compliant manner. SAP is also a founding member of the Enterprise Services Community Process, an organization that invites SAP, its customers, and other independent software vendors to design add-on SAP products. Organized to resemble successful collaborative standards-setting groups such as the Java Community Process and the open-source foundation Eclipse, the Community allows partners and customers to work with SAP to design enterprise services that solve emerging technology and industry problems and—equally important— gain more value from ESA.

Speaking of gaining more value, the topic of creating and promoting industry-wide standards has recurred throughout our exploration of ESA for financial services companies. Having touched this topic so often, it's now time to take a closer look at the important role that standards play in a service-enabled IT environment.

8   ESA: A Framework to Build, Develop, and Run Standards-Based Business Applications

When products meet our expectations, we tend to take it for granted. We are usually unaware of the role played by standards in raising levels of quality, safety, reliability, efficiency, and interchangeability—as well as in providing these benefits at an economical cost.[1]

Standards—in any enterprise, industry, or endeavor—are curious entities. They are all but invisible most of the time, yet, without them, our lives would become enormously complicated. Imagine a world in which newly purchased tires wouldn't fit the wheels of your car, where telephone calls from one country turned to electronic gibberish as they crossed the border, and where TV sets couldn't show programs produced in other regions of the world.

The financial services industry—with its huge transaction volumes and need for cooperation between many different banking and insurance entities—relies on standards as much as (or possibly more than) most other industries. Without standards, it would be quite difficult to transfer funds between accounts, execute an order at a securities exchange, operate an insurance network, or meet the compliance demands of regulatory bodies. Standards, however, do far more than enable basic, repetitive activities like check clearing or claims processing; they also provide a means for banks and insurers to design and build innovative products or services that help create a competitive advantage in the marketplace (at least until the innovations are copied by watchful, fast-moving competitors).

Standards in the financial services industry

It's a fundamental irony of business that standardization leads not to conformity and sameness, but rather to creativity and new ideas. Freed from the laborious task of figuring out the annoying, plumbing-level mechanics and specifications of a business initiative or transaction, senior executives and IT leaders can instead concentrate on dreaming up imaginative products or concepts that can be brought to market quickly.

So standards do matter. A lot. They support faster, more efficient business processes, better customer service, greater interoperability and improved product quality. And, as we implied earlier, companies that are early

Why standards matter

---

1   "Why Standards Matter," International Organization for Standardization (ISO), published at *www.iso.org*.

adopters of an emerging standard have the potential to create a competitive advantage in the marketplace. Standards also have a big impact on merger and acquisition activity; firms that have high adherence to standards are perceived as having substantial value. Companies that don't adhere to key standards come with a lot of baggage, enough, perhaps, to scuttle or hamper an otherwise attractive merger.

When comparing industry usage of standards, it's interesting to note that financial services firms tend to rely on standards primarily in the business-to-business (B2B) environment. One of the reasons for this somewhat narrow applicability appears to be that banks and insurers have not yet reached the level of industrialization or componentization found in other industries (see discussion, in Chapter 2).

Industry norms Let's take a moment to compare financial services with automobile manufacturing. In the auto industry, standardization was first applied to small parts such as light bulbs, piston rings, and safety-buckles—somewhat insignificant parts of larger manufacturing units. Then the larger units themselves—headlights, pistons, and seat belts—became standard components. At this point, auto manufacturers concluded that these items could be made by qualified third-party specialists, thus saving considerable time, money, and invested capital. As outsourcers began to leverage their skills, selling identical (or almost identical) components to multiple manufacturers, unit prices came down even more. The key to this enhanced efficiency and lowered costs? Standards. The outsourcing model works only because all players up and down the value chain agree on commonly applied norms.

Can this model be applied to banks and insurers? In many ways, the answer is yes. Even though they don't manufacture products in a shop-floor environment, financial services firms are increasingly trying to blend current products in novel or imaginative ways. Insurance companies, for example, may seek to combine health policies with property/casualty coverage and offer "family insurance" packages. Banks might want to give "proximity cards" to current savings or checking customers, saving them the trouble of keying in passcodes or waiting for authorizations as they initiate certain transactions or request information.

Interchange-ability of components This sum-of-the-parts-is-greater-than-the-whole approach to product development depends on the interchangeability of the core building blocks. And this compatibility, in turn, is eased by adherence to commonly accepted standards—especially since some pieces of a blended product may come from third-party providers.

8.1 Categories of Standards

All financial services companies rely heavily on IT systems and solutions. Front office, back office, product development, and compliance—there's no corner of the company (other than sweeping floors or brewing coffee, perhaps) that doesn't depend on information technology. When it comes to IT, standards are not only the icing on the cake; they're also the yeast that makes the cake rise.

In general, standards are devised to make sure that products, processes, and knowledge are interoperable or shareable or intelligible. More specifically, standards help financial services firms (and companies in just about all other industries) gain maximum value from their IT landscape. Here's a list of the benefits that standards can produce in an IT architecture:

Benefits of standards

▶ Standards tend to be open and non-proprietary, which means they benefit all parties equally and inhibit one competitor from gaining a stranglehold over segments of the market.

▶ Standards can prevent vendor lock-ins, ensuring that consumers of IT products and services will always enjoy a healthy freedom of choice.

▶ Standards almost always increase the interoperability, portability, connectivity, and transparency of various components of an IT landscape.

▶ Standards focus on the glue, girders, and content of IT architecture (protocols, API's, etc.), but not on the actual implementations. This means that standards usually have a longer lifecycle than IT solutions and versions of these solutions. For example, the description of payment messaging—once it has become a standard—tends to live considerably longer than a release of a payment application.

▶ Use of standards decreases the learning curve within an organization, since many key skills or approaches remain constant even as IT solutions, applications, and components change.

There are three basic groups of standards within an open service-oriented architecture: semantic standards, technology standards, and portability standards (see Figure 8.1). Each of these groups is used at different processing layers for different purposes.

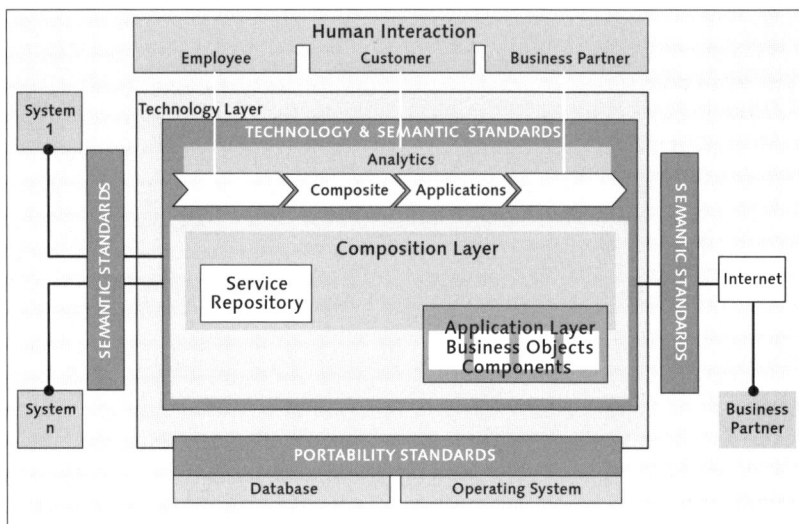

Figure 8.1 Where Standards Apply

8.1.1 Semantic Standards

Assigning meaning to data

Semantic standards enable collaboration by defining what things like *customer*, *invoice*, *payment*, or *claim* actually mean. This, to the surprise of many uninitiated observers, is one of the hardest challenges within an enterprise. Because of disparate data sources, the words *Customer*, *Client*, *Sales Account*, *Business Partner*, and *Party* may all mean the same thing. Conversely, what ought to be a common concept (invoice, for example) may be interpreted in perplexingly different ways at various places inside and outside an enterprise. The *raison d'etre* of semantic standards is to put an end to this uncertainty and ambiguity.

Elements of semantic standards

Semantic standards have two primary elements:

▶ **Data definitions**
They define the format, structure, and meaning of the data that businesses exchange with their customers or with other businesses. These definitions also describe the information exchanged and stored by applications.

▶ **Collaborative process definitions**
These are sometimes called choreography standards, define how two or more businesses work together by delineating the sequence in which documents are exchanged. For example, an invoice sent to a customer should usually result in a payment of the invoiced amount.

Semantic standards are of paramount importance to almost all businesses, because they have the potential to diminish the agony of integrating IT solutions. Not surprisingly, financial services firms and the sector's standards groups are keenly interested in standardizing the definition of messages and their components in order to enlarge the reach of banking and insurance norms. One prominent example is the publication of a harmonized data dictionary for the insurance industry which was created by a coalition of international standards organization that includes ACORD, eEG7, and CSIO. The jointly published compendium houses a set of reusable core components which can serve as a basis for the development of communication messages between all lines of the insurance business, independent of underlying technology. Examples like this one show that the work of like-minded industry organizations can significantly reduce semantic complexity and promote intra-industry collaboration. Semantics become even more important within IT organizations, especially those of larger companies. When a thousand or more people are working on different parts of the IT landscape, jointly forged semantic standards enable the seamless integration of individual accomplishments.

Harmonized data dictionary

8.1.2 Technical Standards

While semantic standards help define the meaning of things like data fields, messages, and objects, technical standards describe (among other things) what needs to be done to enable message exchange within an IT landscape. The difficulty here, for most banks and insurers, is that over time there have been multiple waves of technology innovation: new programming languages, databases, operating systems, user interface tools, data warehouses, Enterprise Application Integration (EAI) tools, and so forth. Each of these innovations arrived with its own lexicon of technology standards, and each has made its way into the development and runtime environment. Here, they tend to remain. (Just as in a notable U.S. television commercial about a trap for cockroaches, "They check in, but they don't check out!") As a resultConseq, virtually every IT landscape includes solutions, components, and applications built on different underlying technologies. Almost all of them are still useful and will, no doubt, be around for some time. This means that one of the most important tasks for the business software community is to support SOA's basic requirement for technology independence by establishing and promoting technology standards that enable integration between IT solutions built on differing principles.

Enabling message exchange

Enterprise services architecture can be quite helpful in harmonizing this eclectic aggregation of IT building blocks. Building on existing SOA and Web services standards, ESA serves as a comprehensive stack of all standards that are important for developing and running business solutions. This includes not only the identification and selection of existing standards, but also the change processes that are required to incorporate standards into a given IT landscape, and—where required—a managed approach to enhancing standards over time.

8.1.3 Portability Standards

Independence from operating systems

Portability is an attribute of a computer program that can be used in operating system other than the one in which it was created, without requiring major adaptation. Portability standards have been developed to help applications achieve an optimum amount of independence from the operating systems and databases on which they run. This interchangeability is achieved by introducing a dedicated architectural layer between the operating system/database environment and the solutions. This layer typically includes an application server, which acts as a kind of universal translator and lubricant for messages moving up and down the technology stack. Enterprise services architecture brings new power and agility to this abstraction seam, providing a framework to ensure that applications built on top of diverse technologies can move easily between different operating systems and databases.

8.2 Standards in Enterprise Services Architecture

Standards in SOA

With the above—admittedly very condensed—classification in mind, the question now is how to best benefit from standards in a service-based architecture. Although all of the abovementioned categories are important, semantic standards can be said to have the greatest impact; studies have shown that up to 95% of the cost of building connections between systems is spent on clarifying semantics and business logic. There are two reasons for this. First, integrations force business and IT leaders to spend a great deal of time and money deciding on clear definitions for business objects that will be processed by the linked applications. In addition, since hitherto-independent applications often have overlapping capabilities, the integration team has to set limits on where processing should begin and end. The former task, however, requires most of the heavy lifting; if semantics are standardized across the enterprise (or even across the value chain), integration costs can be reduced significantly.

Does service-oriented architecture help here? The answer is yes, but with some qualification. Generic SOA provides only technical guidance where Web services are concerned; it does not address the need for the kind of semantic standardization required to enable maximum benefits. That said, there have been a number of efforts to overcome the deficiencies. One such effort can be traced back to the dawn of generic SOA's basic architecture and the blooming of available services in all IT areas, both within companies and in public areas. This development sounds encouraging at first, but a closer look reveals some challenges. When the modeling of services is done in an unsupervised manner by the creators of provider services and the creators of consumer services, the former have a natural advantage, because they themselves determine the functional scope of their services. For this reason, having control over the provider service very often implies that the creator of the service defines the functional scope, whereas consumers have no choice but to "take it or leave it." Consequently, the functional scope of a provider service often fits only a few consumers, or, in extreme cases, just one. This limits the reuse-potential of a service rather drastically.

The need to balance service providers and consumers

One way to overcome this problem is to give both parties a "right to speak," which is the approach used by many standardization bodies. While this approach has proven successful in many cases, it, too, comes with some baggage. It takes a long time for the various parties to come to an agreement, and it takes even more time for an approved standard to make its way into productive use. The major issue here is that standardization institutions tend to take their mission very seriously; they have a tendency to get carried away, taking standardization to its maximum level. Although this sounds like a good idea—especially in commonly accepted areas where productivity gains are the main goal—there's a danger that the opportunities for subsequent innovation can be strangled. For example, if all the attributes of a message are fixed, a bank or insurance company can distinguish itself by content only. Under these circumstances, it's hard (or even impossible) to introduce new business features that help a company differentiate itself from the competition.

What Are the Consequences?

There is little or no doubt about the value of standardization bodies. Their inherent balancing mechanisms create solutions that meet the needs of divergent interests, even if the adjudication process tends to take a long time. Standards groups are making impressive progress in many areas. On the integration front, there are several promising developments, includ-

Standardization bodies

ing initiatives brought to life by the International Organization for Standardization (ISO) and the UN/CEFACT Technologies and Methodologies Group (TMG). Examples include:

▶ Core Components Technical Specification (CCTS), which provides precise semantic definitions for business documents and processes

▶ Naming and Design Rules (NDR) that specify how the core components developed by CCTS (such as address, full name, or line item) can be mapped consistently to XML

Degree of standardization

However, integration issues can only be solved with a solid understanding of the business concerns behind them. Equally important, the degree of standardization must be set correctly: high enough to create efficiency, but not so high as to stifle differentiation. No one is suggesting that the IT community should roll back the wheel, give up on SOA's "black box" approach and recreate the era of standardized data models (an approach that didn't work very well the first time around). Instead, those who set standards must simultaneously evaluate all relevant areas—data, functions, business processes, and integration—in order to establish a degree of standardization that provides support for most, if not all, enterprises in the financial services industry.

Industry-wide acceptance

To this end, SAP, like many other companies, has been doing some groundwork. ESA describes the fundamental building blocks—*enterprise services* and the *messages* to integrate them, *components* that bundle enterprise services with a view to business tasks, *deployment units*, made up of components that have a common lifecycle and therefore are deployed together, and domains, which serve as a high-level structuring element to align software solutions with business responsibilities. These elements have been designed based on experience gained from many successful software installations. Additionally, they benefit from new, promising innovations like SOA and other state-of-the art innovations. But, without industry-wide acceptance, all this would amount to yet another innovation cycle—one that might run the risk of flaming out quickly, like so many of its predecessors. This is why SAP is committed to supporting the services evolution process through ongoing dialogue with standardization bodies in the financial services and IT industries.

SAP has launched a number of initiatives to foster standardization in key areas. These include:

▶ Architecture forums with chief architects of major banks and insurance companies on topics such as business and technology architectures, process standards, business semantics, definition of and migration paths to target architectures.

▶ The Industry Value Network for Banks, comprising C-level IT banking executives and chief architects of leading international banks, who jointly with SAP define the banking-specific enterprise services required to make SOA a reality for the banking industry.

These initiatives are not intended to compete with existing efforts. The goal here is to invite enterprises to exchange information, to share real-world experiences, and to understand SOA best practices so that future standards can evolve more easily. As more and more players in the industry open their cookbooks, others will follow with attractive recipes, and the industry, as a whole, will profit.

Conclusion: Enterprise services architecture serves as a framework on which companies can develop, build, and run standards-based business applications that support innovative, cost-effective, and profitable business processes. SAP plays an active role in creating, promoting, and accepting industrial and technical IT standards that help financial services move down the path to a service-enabled architecture.

In the next chapters, we'll look at some of the stepping stones with which that path is paved.

Note to the reader: Although this chapter focuses mainly on semantic standards, it is important to notice the significant role of the following standards groups:

▶ W3C—develops XML, XML Schema, XSLT, WSDL, and more (SAP is a gold-level sponsor of the Web Accessibility Initiative [WAI] and a member of the W3C Advisory Board that provides strategy-level guidance to the W3C management team.)

▶ OASIS—develops standards such as WS BPEL and WS Notification (SAP is a member of the OASIS Board that directs OASIS activities.)

▶ WS-I—develops profiles of how service-oriented architecture, XML, and Web services standards should be used together

▶ Java Community Process—controls the development of the Java language

▶ Eclipse Foundation—manages the development of the Eclipse development environment

▶ Object Management Group (OMG)—develops the model-driven architecture (MDA), the Unified Modeling Language (UML), the MetaObject Facility (MOF), and the XML Metadata Interchange (XMI)

▶ Liberty Alliance—develops standards for managing identity on the Web

▶ DMTF—develops management standards for integration technology and Internet environments

9   Making the Move: How to Handle the Transition to ESA

The journey to an enterprise services architecture (ESA) will depend, in one sense, on tangible actions and activities: harmonizing business processes, decoupling user interfaces, and making business objects and services accessible through open, standards-based access mechanisms. This work will, of course, be challenging. But the more difficult task lies in programming the special computers that lie between the ears of business and IT leaders. In other words, the real starting point for the transition to ESA is in the hearts and minds of management, and not in lines of code, solution maps, or process models.

With this in mind, let's look at six key success factors that can fill some of the potholes and eliminate the dead ends on the road to ESA. Figure 9.1 summarizes the transition roadmap to ESA.

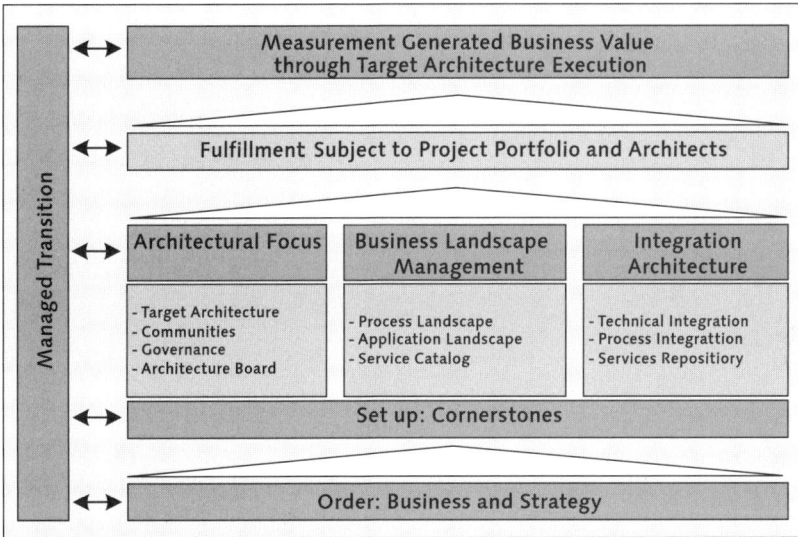

Figure 9.1 Transition Roadmap

9.1   Success Factor No. 1: Decide Where You're Going and Why You're Going There

It has been said—perhaps a few times too many—that every journey begins with a single step. While this may be true enough, there's very little point in taking even that single step if you don't know where you're heading. This is a roundabout way of saying that common sense plays (or

A motive and a map

should play) a large role in the transition to service-oriented architecture. Since this particular journey will undoubtedly last for several years and consume a fair amount of time and resources, it's a good idea to make sure that the trip is justifiable and quantifiable. For most financial services firms, this means making sure there's a motive and a map.

9.1.1 A Motive

Business reasons Companies that sail through uncharted waters and reach their SOA goals generally have a compelling business reason for undertaking the voyage. These reasons vary considerably, but what they have in common is a certain urgency and intensity. Reducing costs is a common goal, as is consolidation of duplicated resources after a merger. Other compelling drivers include launching a new business strategy or integrating new sales channels. Whatever the goal—operational or strategic—it often emerges as a company senses that a gun has been placed against its head. Shareholders, customers, or regulators may be so frustrated, or competitors may be gaining ground so ruthlessly, that senior managers set aside any reservations and commit to a new architecture. This support and focus is very important; companies with unclear motives or inconsistent commitment find it difficult to orchestrate change or allocate budget resources.

9.1.2 A Map

Target IT landscape To ensure consistent decision-making and lasting change, financial services firms need a clear understanding of the kind of IT landscape toward which they are striving. The target architecture, as we'll see below, does not need to be a dense, tech-laden compendium of specifications and code provisions. Instead, it should serve as a kind of bible, or vision statement, or wish list—a surprisingly brief, descriptive document that outlines the key principles and governance issues that will shape development and deployment of the service-oriented architecture. The goal is to provide reference points and alignment for all the people who will build and benefit from the new architecture. A target IT landscape enables all IT project managers and architects to set priorities in daily business; it prevents conflict and overlap even though a hundred parallel projects may be moving ahead simultaneously.

Detours Of course, in real life, nothing actually works that smoothly. Exceptions arise, innovations emerge as new efficiencies are realized, turf wars smolder. To deal with these and similar issues, it's best to avoid relying on maverick architectural methods (those outside the scope of the target architecture), because they carry a risk (i.e., the coding and connectors can get buried deep in the technology stack, and then become forgotten as memories dim and staffs turn over). So flexibility is important; companies will always want to deviate slightly from the target architecture when there's a good reason for doing so. The solution is to build in a certain amount of tolerance for valuable detours—to consciously allow architectural exceptions for worthy projects while vetoing course corrections that add little value. The key is to make sure that changes are visible, open, and well documented—that they become part of the fabric of the architecture, and not oddball patches and fixes, which soon disappear from sight.

> **Conclusion:** If you intend to make the transition to enterprise services architecture, make sure that you have a compelling reason for doing so and a clear idea of what you want the architecture to look like.

9.2 Success Factor No. 2: Do Not Try the "Great Leap Forward" Approach

With map and motive in hand, let's now take that infamous first step of the journey toward an ESA. Lest anyone be tempted to take one giant step, remember that virtually all financial services companies have concluded that an existing IT landscape cannot be improved by a "big bang" overhaul of the architecture. (Actually, this approach *could* work, but only if a company was willing to shut down its systems for a year and support business processes manually during the changeover.) Clearly, the favored transition policy emphasizes the use of periodic, incremental steps. Let's call this approach "managed transition."

Managed transition typically produces gradual improvement, while maintaining a balance between short- and mid-term goals. The strategy also helps to resolve the conflicts that inevitably arise when functional needs clash with architectural goals. The idea is to fix a small, digestible piece of the IT infrastructure, and then move on to the next. Visibility is a key characteristic of this process. If, along the way, a repair is managed using techniques not found in the repair manual, as it were, then the departure must be noted and incorporated into the manual so that everyone can find it or refer to it in the future.

Managed transition

Managed transition also helps keep business and IT architecture improvements in balance. If quick system fixes are made to support pressing business needs, the architecture suffers. If too much energy is spent on IT plumbing alone, there is little payoff at the business level. Of course, like any other corporate initiative, managed transition works only when influential people support it. The conversion to a new IT architecture—and to its successful implementation—must be embraced and funded, and buttressed organizationally and procedurally. The transition is likely to fail if it does not have complete buy-in from IT leaders, line of business leaders, and senior management.

> **Conclusion:** Managed transition helps financial services companies move toward ESA one step at a time, while maintaining a healthy balance between business needs and architectural needs.

9.3 Success Factor No. 3: Elevate the Status of Your IT Architecture

Traditionally, architecture hasn't received much respect or attention in financial services companies. From an IT perspective, some firms may be said to have a project focus or application focus, but very few enterprises put architecture at the center of their world. However, to make a successful transition to ESA, it's necessary to bring architecture into focus and to confer upon it a higher level of importance and value.

Executive sponsors Architecture needs sponsors and stakeholders. It also needs a governing body with the power to give orders, determine a budget, set the key performance indicators (KPIs) with which progress will be measured, and determine the responsibilities needed for execution. Firms that have recognized the importance of this activity tend to establish architecture boards, which are typically chaired by a chief technology architect but also include business architects and project managers. (It's not unheard of for a CIO, CEO, or head of a line of business to serve as the board's executive sponsor.) The board is held accountable for the target architecture. It adopts guidelines, checks compliance with these guidelines, and resolves conflicts of interest as they arise. For example, if a project team determines that its needs will exceed a budgeted figure by 10%, but the project leader is unwilling to exceed the budget allotment, someone will have to settle this dispute. As discussed above, it is important that exceptions are made consciously and transparently, and that there are clear responsibilities for the step-by-step progress toward a target architecture.

The architecture board plays a central role, but with only a handful of people serving on the board, there's a limit to the amount of day-to-day oversight, management, and control of various projects. With many large financial services firms handling up to 2,000 projects at a time, micro-management from the board would create a dangerous bottleneck. That's why the setting of guidelines is so important; it confers enough power on architects to solve most problems on their own, approaching the board only under preordained circumstances. Another way to reduce potential conflict is to make sure that the architecture reporting line is independent from the project reporting line. SAP, for example, has established an architecture board that includes chief architects and senior managers as the decision-making body. Not only does the board proactively set guidelines and priorities, it also supports development projects by making decisions about how architectural conflicts can be resolved.

Setting guidelines

Since fulfillment of the target architecture is part of development, an architecture board (at SAP or any other company) must establish and promote clear governance processes, guidelines, and KPIs. The governance guidelines tend to be somewhat like the Ten Commandments in that they are brief, authoritative, and far-reaching. For example, a guideline might read as follows: "Layers of responsibility (UI layer, process layer, and business object layer) must be decoupled from each other."

Governance guidelines and KPIs

Another example: "Customer contact centers must be independent of the operating system." Or "In- and outsourcing of operating applications should not limit the accounting and compliance capabilities". Key performance indicators, on the other hand, are far more specific. Examples might include the number of services to be implemented and used within the first year, or the number of functional areas that have been decoupled. Another KPI can be the time and effort required to use an existing service compared to former projects (e.g. connecting a new channel). While the number of KPIs will vary greatly, depending on company characteristics and goals, a financial services firm might use between 10 and 50 during the early phase of the transition.

Enterprise services architecture relies on a mutual understanding of business fundamentals—a common language that can be used to describe cross-enterprise activities such as clearing, payments, transfers, and a host of other processes. To establish these homogeneous semantics, the architecture board—or its designees—must actively participate in community-building activities within the financial services industry.

Conclusion: An architectural focus is critical for an ongoing implementation of ESA, and this focus must be reflected in the organizational structure of banks and insurers.

9.4 Success Factor No. 4: Change the Way You Manage Your Business Landscape Lifecycle

With monolithic, tightly coupled systems, most of which have grown by accretion, the concept of lifecycle management has barely been applicable. Depending on business needs, enterprises tend to keep fixing and patching their applications more or less indefinitely. This has made the notion of a new release almost irrelevant in many cases, especially with analytic backend systems. When change is called for, the IT staff—typically assisted by systems integration consultants—creates the improvements, and then makes laborious changes to all the areas impacted by the new functionality.

Business landscape lifecycle With ESA the management of the IT environment will be considerably easier, thanks to independent business logic, service-enabled components, fixed boundaries between application functionality, and services based on commonly accepted standards. This will result in a business landscape lifecycle—a beneficial environment in which individual pieces of the system can be upgraded or replaced with minimal disruption to the IT infrastructure or supported business processes. Portfolios will become independent, while business processes, applications, and services can all evolve as needed, at whatever pace generates the greatest benefit.

Still, this won't happen automatically. It will require consistent effort. Business logic will need to be extracted from EAI-linked components before being standardized and consolidated. New versions of processes, applications, and interfaces will have to be designed, implemented, and monitored. Decisions will have to be made about where business redundancy exists and how to eliminate it. All of this will require teamwork among owners of application domains as service providers, service consumers, and architects—who keep standards alive by applying the architectural guidelines and KPIs established by the architecture board.

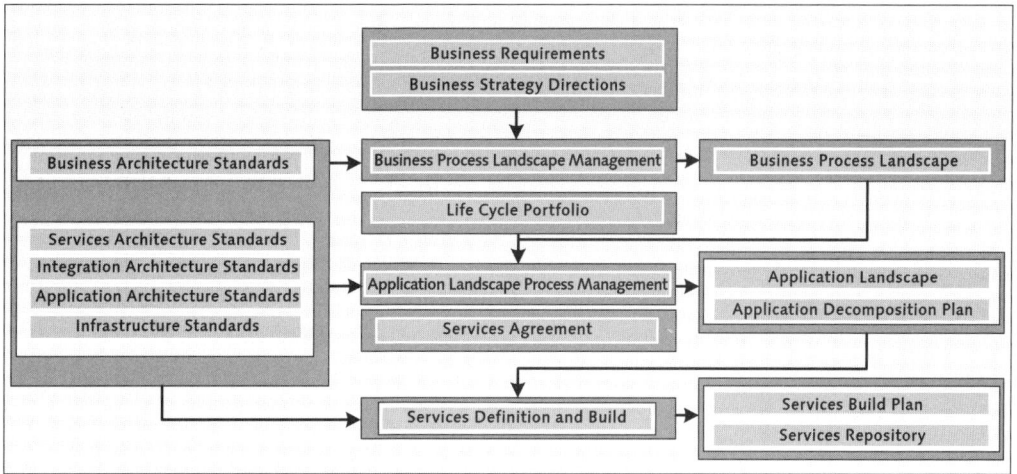

Figure 9.2 Business Landscape Lifecycle and Portfolio Management

As shown in Figure 9.2, fulfillment of the target architecture will first deal with the decomposition of applications, then address the building of services. The overall business landscape management will also require new descriptions of the decoupled application layers, namely:

▶ The business process landscape

▶ The application landscape and portfolio

▶ The service catalogue/repository

Conclusion: ESA requires—but also supports—a new way of managing the business landscape lifecycle and the processes, applications, and services therein.

9.5 Success Factor No. 5: Don't Neglect Integration Architecture

In addition to philosophical or business-oriented guidelines and decisions, the journey toward ESA also depends on building the right technology infrastructure. In the course of deploying a service-oriented architecture, with its decomposed and decoupled landscape, questions will arise regarding communication techniques, security, and system performance.

Enterprise services architecture that properly reflects a company's business priorities requires an infrastructure capable of managing services, user interactions, and automated processes. Little by little, tightly cou-

Integration infra-
structure

pled, monolithic systems, complete with their hidden business logic and process management, will be replaced by loosely coupled service providers. The integration infrastructure will manage this process, ensuring that services are executed and exceptions are monitored. An additional challenge is managing the technical integration between design time and runtime: to what degree should the modeling of processes and services be integrated in the runtime environment? And still another challenge is version management and transport management; as new releases and upgrades come along, it becomes much harder to monitor and manage them, and preserve quality and efficiency in the runtime environment.

Banks and insurers making the transition to ESA will gain considerable freedom of choice when it comes to lifecycle management, but they will still have to make decisions about updating, improving, or retiring a wide range of processes, applications, and services. SAP Solution Manager is one way to deal with these issues. This tool is used to manage solutions, starting at the business-scenario level and working down through different methods to service consumers and service providers. SAP Solution Manager facilitates technical support for distributed systems, and also includes functionality that covers key aspects of solution design, deployment, test, operation, and continuous improvement. Offered as part of SAP NetWeaver and included in the annual maintenance fee for SAP solutions, the toolset has been used by a number of customers to ensure that their entire SAP solution environment is living up to its potential.

> **Conclusion:** Integration architecture is important for efficient implementation and management of the IT landscape and the ESA-powered communication approach. In an ESA environment, integration architecture ensures that business drivers, processes, and goals are plugged directly into IT.

9.6 Success Factor No. 6: Know Where You're Going, When You Get There, and How to Measure Whether the Trip Did You Any Good

ESA Adoption Program

The transition to ESA depends on many decisions, some of which should be made up front, and some of which will be made as needed in the future. To support this multifaceted evolution, software providers typically offer a number of support tools and consultative programs. SAP's offering in this area in known as the ESA Adoption Program, a formalized yet flexible methodology that simplifies the journey toward a service-oriented architecture by turning it into a series of logical steps (see Figure 9.3). As part of the program, SAP provides valuable tools such as workshops, templates, content, and other services. This blend of methodology and supporting tools streamlines and simplifies the transition to ESA, helping financial services firms find answers to the following general questions:

▶ What are the business issues that drive the deployment of ESA?

▶ Which processes, domains, and applications will be involved?

▶ What will the actual ESA implementation look like?

▶ What steps need to be taken, in what order, and how long will it take?

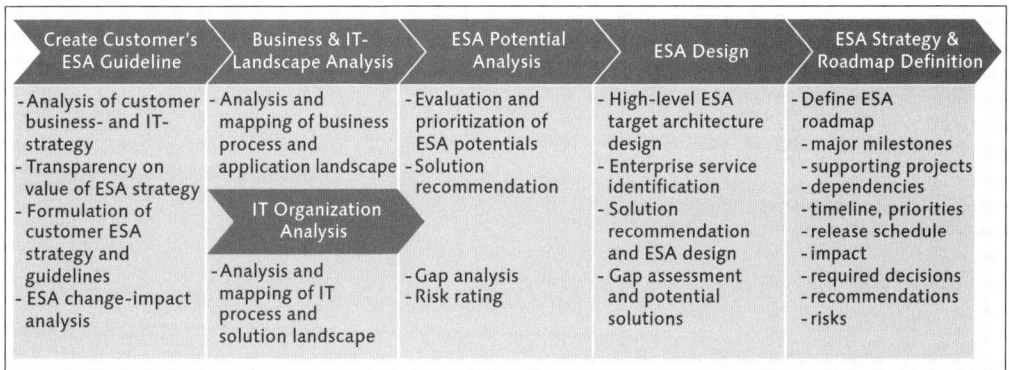

Create Customer's ESA Guideline	Business & IT-Landscape Analysis	ESA Potential Analysis	ESA Design	ESA Strategy & Roadmap Definition
- Analysis of customer business- and IT-strategy - Transparency on value of ESA strategy - Formulation of customer ESA strategy and guidelines - ESA change-impact analysis	- Analysis and mapping of business process and application landscape **IT Organization Analysis** - Analysis and mapping of IT process and solution landscape	- Evaluation and prioritization of ESA potentials - Solution recommendation - Gap analysis - Risk rating	- High-level ESA target architecture design - Enterprise service identification - Solution recommendation and ESA design - Gap assessment and potential solutions	- Define ESA roadmap - major milestones - supporting projects - dependencies - timeline, priorities - release schedule - impact - required decisions - recommendations - risks

Figure 9.3 ESA Adoption Programm

As financial services firms make the transition to an ESA, each step, each decision, each detour, and each implementation needs to be monitored and, where possible, measured. Key performance indicators that pertain to the use of services and the reuse of business logic must be established and communicated. The overall process depends on a recurring loop of assessment, design, implementation, and monitoring.

Conclusion: Like all other projects in any company, anywhere, a transition to ESA has to generate business value. ESA is a broad, somewhat perplexing topic, and it will be approached quite differently, depending on the resources, strategy, and outlook of a given company. Reaching the value-creation goal depends on drawing up clear plans, using valid yardsticks, and applying lessons learned in one project to what's about to happen in the next.

To summarize and conclude this chapter, the transition to ESA will be arduous but not necessarily agonizing; detailed but not necessarily diabolical; comprehensive but not necessarily confounding. And the payoff—new levels of adaptability, flexibility, and openness—makes this particular transition well worth the effort.

10   ESA Checklist: The Steps to be Taken

In Chapter 9, we discussed success factors that will help banks and insurers make a smooth transition to a service-enabled IT landscape. While critically important, these factors don't necessarily result in an action plan. If the goal is to create and migrate to a target architecture, it's not a good idea to jump right in and start service-enabling current applications willy-nilly. The preferred approach is to invest some time up front — laying out the steps in an ESA transition chart, before digging down into technical details. Careful planning and preparation can prevent setbacks in the latter phases of such projects, especially when they span the entire enterprise.

As shown in Figure 10.1 below, the journey to ESA can be divided into four major phases: preparation, planning, execution, and the accompanying organizational adaptations (not only within the enterprise, but also in the business partner ecosystem). While these phases flow in a logical order, many companies will skip or even repeat certain steps based on the circumstances of a given project or the amount of work that may already have been accomplished.

The journey to ESA

Step	Activity	Phase
1	Identify business drivers	Prepare
2	Define game rules	
3	Understand differentiators	Plan
4	Map context systems	
5	Create a dual roadmap for consolidation and composition	
6	Sort out master data	Execution
7	Prioritize based on severity of event-cost clusters	
8	Create a new dictionary	
9	Connect the dots	
10	Create skill centers	Organize
11	Build an IT organization that looks at the business as a whole	
12	Externalize and connect to your network of partners	

Figure 10.1 Twelve Steps Towards ESA

10.1 Phase 1: Prepare

Identify business drivers

In the past, many worthwhile projects have started with an IT focus, addressing seemingly obvious architectural problems, and then failed. There are any number of reasons for such collapses, but one major culprit is a narrow focus; in far too many cases, the benefits of an IT restructuring are clear to IT leaders only, which means that business leaders are reluctant to support the cause.

ESA, with its top-down, business-driven design and deployment approach, can help to overcome this problem, since business owners, of necessity, must be involved in a fair amount of the upfront work and will therefore be aware of the business benefits that are likely to flow from IT enhancements. Successful transition to ESA depends on being crystal clear about which business issues are being addressed and what the benefits will be. To ensure overall success, there is arguably no step more important than identifying the business drivers at the beginning of the process.

Clearly, this requires a collaborative approach, one that depends on detailed discussions between business and IT leaders, involving relevant stakeholders from both areas. To prevent misunderstandings, it's a good idea to establish common ground rules; these include defining responsibilities, setting up lines of communication, establishing a framework for tracking results, and using project metrics as inputs for the steps to follow.

10.2 Phase 2: Plan

Key competences

Once all stakeholders are on board and the guidelines are laid out, it's time to develop a plan. Which systems will benefit most from service-enablement and what are the expected outcomes of actually doing the work? The first step in the planning phase, however, is not to start hunting for antiquated or inefficient systems, but to gain a better understanding of what makes the enterprise unique. What are the skills, processes, activities, or systems that create a competitive advantage versus those that simply help keep the doors open? There may be multiple answers to questions like these, and they will more than likely relate to both IT and business. The point here is that a successful transition to ESA depends on making a concerted effort to identify the areas that attract customers, fatten margins, and drive market leadership.

As described by author and business consultant Geoffrey Moore, these mission-critical areas are often referred to as *core*, while other necessary but less vital areas are referred to as *context*.[1] Here's a caveat relating to context: be careful. Treating certain processes as context does not mean that you can ignore or neglect them. Context areas—and their related IT systems—are important because they affect profitability and efficiency, even if they don't result in a competitive edge. Within IT, context may include legacy systems, redundant systems left over from earlier consolidations, or systems that have had their functionality supplanted by newer resources. Whatever the reason, they're perhaps ready for a major housecleaning. As a general rule, context systems need a different strategy than that used for core areas, and therefore each requires its own roadmap. For example, a bank or insurer may decide to concentrate on realizing productivity gains in context areas, instead of investing in additional features and functions. This approach may ultimately result in a decision to replace outmoded systems with commoditized tools or even to outsource them.

The core and context model

This overall planning phase—which includes making decisions about the potential use of commodity tools, standard software packages, and outsourcing—is quite a departure for any bank or insurance company that has historically relied on in-house development. If this is the case, the people planning or executing IT projects may require different skills compared with self-development specialists. This necessity is causing a transformation in the role of IT architects, who must now establish close relationships with their counterparts in many different areas of the business. The goal: to recognize commonalities, identify best practices, and make informed decisions about where an enterprise can benefit from self-development and where money might be better spent on partner solutions. Consequently, today's architects need broad insight into partner (and outsourced) offerings in order to assess the opportunities and risks associated with any make-or-buy decision.

Make or buy?

10.3   Phase 3: Execution

With a prioritized list of architecture projects at hand, the planning phase gives way to execution. An important first step in landscape optimization is to reduce and unify the master data environment (the systems that hold information describing accounts, customers, vendors, parties, orga-

Master data

---

1 Geoffrey Moore, *Inside the Tornado: Marketing Strategies from Silicon Valley's Cutting Edge*, (HarperBusiness, 1999).

nizational structures, etc.). As outlined in Chapter 6, the optimization process should result in a landscape with fewer instances for master data management—a landscape where redundancy is permitted only when it cannot be avoided. ESA can be of substantial benefit here, as one of its most salient virtues is that it helps enterprises abstract data, processes, business objects, components, and so forth in one virtual location—eliminating the integration headaches that result when data is locked rigidly into a single place or spread too thin in many places.

Landscape assessment The second step in the ESA execution phase is to take a close look at other parts of the landscape. "Taking a close look" means assessing a project's importance (as determined by the core/context yardstick) along with its cost. Note that cost assessments should definitely be based on potential changes to both software and hardware; the virtualization concepts of ESA help move data out of redundant servers, which can then be retired. This means that banks and insurers have the option of breaking the expensive habit of using one server for each system.

Enterprise Services Repository With the optimized landscape at hand, the next step is to determine which services each of the components should provide and which services they will consume. As outlined in Chapter 6, this exercise begins with an analysis of business processes, and then moves down to the component landscape. At this point, some kind of register is needed—a surveyable location for services. SAP's version of this dictionary is the Enterprise Services Repository—an aggregation point and reference library for services from every corner of the enterprise.

After the functionality has been abstracted from hard-coded applications, you will begin to see how yesterday's integration solutions can be replaced with out-of-the-box solutions or components from SAP and other providers. At this stage, it's likely that architects and business leaders will also gain an understanding of how a well designed enterprise service can be used and reused, supporting processes in multiple product areas and lines of business. This connect-the-dots exercise reveals the true value of ESA, which becomes apparent only as services are recycled. If this does not occur, the time and effort of transitioning to ESA will have been wasted. Luckily, once enterprise services have been designed and deployed, they can be leveraged across all corners of the corporation (see Chapter 7 for more information). Let's say, for example, that a bank or insurer creates services called *account opening*, *product configuration*, or *output management*. These generic activities can be utilized on behalf of virtually any product, business line, or sales channel. The service itself does not know or care what products or accounts or data it is handling; all it knows is how to combine things.

10.4 Phase 4: Organize

As described above, the execution phase includes several steps that are taken during the implementation of a service-enabled landscape. These steps, as well as the activities that support them, tend to be quite different from each other. They may also require new skills, new processes, and new ways of thinking. For this reason, making a successful transition to ESA often depends on making changes in an IT organization so it can handle new and different tasks. (One of these changes—the evolving role and skill set of IT architects—was cited above as part of our discussion of the planning phase.)

Once ESA-enabling gathers momentum, many parts of the IT organization will be affected. For example, depending on the size of the clusters within core and context areas, it's usually a good idea to set up a dedicated team to guide the consolidation of the existing landscape and another team to oversee the creation and composition of new services and components. For large or complex IT environments, yet another team could be established to act as keepers of the service repository in order to ensure the smoothest possible interaction between providers and consumers. Additionally, if an enterprise depends on cutting-edge innovation, it may even be advisable to create a dedicated research group consisting of creative thinkers who are best equipped to help the enterprise cope with disruptive market forces.

Teamwork

Whatever strategies are used for managing teams, skill sets, or new IT processes, one constant should rule the decision-making process: IT solutions exist to support business efforts. Consequently, IT needs to look beyond its departmental borders, measuring each landscape enhancement in terms of whatever improvement, consolidation, or velocity can be mustered to support operational or strategic goals.

Finally, it's clear that doing business today depends on new levels of trust and cooperation with external partners. This fact must also be reflected in the IT organization. It is not enough to optimize an IT landscape so that it runs smoothly within the four walls of the enterprise. Service-oriented architectures like ESA reach their full potential only when they are externalized and connected to the partner network.

External partners

10.5 Breaking the Silo Stranglehold

Change in a
single action

By following the above checklist, banks and insurers can "flexible-ize" their operations, which today are too often held hostage by monolithic systems. ESA can be the force that breaks the silo stranglehold. In yesterday's landscape, if an accounting rule was changed in one system, it would require a Herculean effort to go into all the other systems and perform the same task. With ESA, a change can be syndicated to all the appropriate areas as the result of a single action. In yesterday's landscape, different parts of the organization would make different determinations of the same question—such as calculating the net present value of a loan. In yesterday's landscape, whoever asked a question would get at least two different answers, or, in order to guarantee a single answer, a horde of people would labor in a back office to reconcile data. With ESA, financial services firms gain the opportunity to create a single version of the truth, no matter where that truth resides or who inquires about it.

Conclusion: As noted throughout these pages, virtually all banks and insurance companies face white-knuckle challenges stemming from the need to deal with (or benefit from) consolidation, industrialization, compliance, and innovation. No one's standing still on any of these fronts, but financial services firms that turn IT into a strategic advantage—instead of a support tool—have a better than average chance of surviving the gathering storm.

Enterprise services architecture has the potential to put IT at the head of the charge, because it leverages and enhances the power of Web services to align IT with business needs. The result is an agile infrastructure that enables fast, efficient development and the ability to orchestrate services, compose them into new applications, and put them to work where they will do the most good for customers, employees, and shareholders.

A   Glossary

Analytics and monitoring service
Type of service to consolidate and store data at the point in time when it first emerges in order to make it available to analytical tasks

Business component
see: Functional Business Component

Business object (BO)
Object-oriented view of data structures, which are composed in order to support functions that cover business tasks

Component service
Type of service monitoring complex relationships between business objects

Compound service
Service that consumes other services in order to provide a result. Enterprise services normally are compound services.

Create, Retrieve, Update, and Delete service (CRUD Service)
Generic service providing basic functions for the creation, retrieval, update, or deletion of business objects. CRUD services are typically utilized within user interfaces, where fast, synchronous communication with small increments of an interaction is needed.

Deployment unit
Group of components that are deployed and used together because of a common business background

Enterprise application integration (EAI)
Collective name applying to several methodologies for the integration of heterogeneous IT landscapes

Enterprise service
Type of service: an interface to well-defined functionality provided by a business component. The interface defines a set of service operations that perform work and can receive and send messages. Enterprise services are used by other programs that consume the services. Services are loosely coupled with the entities that consume their functionality and to each other.

Enterprise services repository

Design-time repository of service objects for enterprise services architecture. These objects include:

▶ Business objects

▶ Service interfaces (with associated operations, message types, and data types)

▶ Business process models

▶ Business scenario and business process objects

Functional business component

Software entity that groups related enterprise services

Process service

Type of service that triggers and manages the execution of a business process or a business process step

Engine service

Type of service providing access to a certain function such as a calculation

Entity service

Type of service providing access to the data of an entity, typically a business object

Global data types (GDT)

Attributes (such as name, address) defined on the basis of the Core Components Technical Specification (CCTS, approved by the UN/CEFACT Technologies and Methodologies Group (TMG), providing precise semantic definitions for business documents and processes

Service

An exposed piece of functionality with three properties:

▶ The interface contract to the service is platform-independent.

▶ The service can be dynamically located and invoked.

▶ The service is self-contained, that is, the service maintains its own state.

Throughout this book, the term "service" is used as a genus for different types of services, especially enterprise services.

Service operation

Executable functionality, described in the interface to a service. Usually a service comprises several service operations, each performing a different task.

Service-oriented architecture (SOA)

This book builds on the following generic definition: service-oriented architecture is a software architecture that supports the design, development, identification, and consumption of standardized services, thereby improving the reusability of software components and creating agility in responding to change.

System of services

Group of enterprise services designed to work together to solve ambitious business tasks

Utility service

Type of service providing frequently used functions for other services

Web service

Type of service built on top of well-known and platform-independent protocols such as HTTP, XML, UDDI, WSDL, and SOAP

Index

Technology standards 95
Third-party provider 64
Top-down approach 59
Total cost of ownership (TCO) 90
Transaction support 73
Transition to ESA 103
Transparency 36, 95

U

UDDI 42
UN/CEFACT Technologies and Metho-
  dologies Group (TMG) 100
Unified environment 92
User environment 69
User interface 67
User interface layer 51
User productivity 68, 71
Utility service 66, 67, 121

V

Validation 67
Valuation 90
Value help 67
Value-adding services 60
Vendor solution 83

W

W3C 102
Waterfall model 49
Web service 14, 29, 30, 41, 42, 57, 59,
  63, 98, 99, 121
WSDL 42
WS-I 102

X

XML 100
XML schema 51

Uncover the real-world applications of the Balanced Scorecard and SAP CPM

Gain practical information about the Management Cockpit, creating scorecards, crucial tips, tricks, and more

Up to date for SEM 6.0

387 pp., 2006, 69,95 Euro / US $69.95
ISBN 978-1-59229-085-7

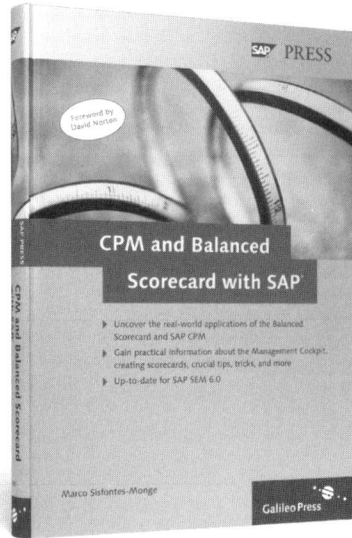

CPM and Balanced Scorecard with SAP

www.sap-press.com

Marco Sisfontes-Monge, Marco Sisfontes-Monge

CPM and Balanced Scorecard with SAP

Organizations planning to initiate the implementation of SAP CPM, using the Balanced Scorecard approach, need this practical guide. Get a clear understanding of the Balanced Scorecard and its relationship with SAP CPM, while gaining a thorough knowledge of the central concepts of both. With a foreword by Dr. David Norton, this book includes practical information about the management cockpit and teaches you how to create SAP CPM scorecards.

**A practical guide
to implementing and using
SAP xApp Analytics**

**Easily deploy, configure, and
combine analytic applications
to customize SAP xApp
Analytics for your needs**

408 pp., 2006, 69,95 Euro / US$ 69.95
ISBN 978-1-59229-102-1

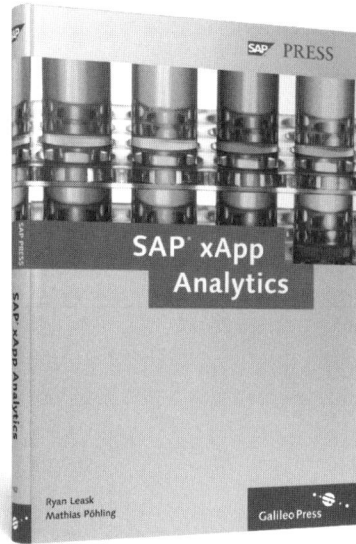

SAP xApp Analytics

www.sap-press.com

Ryan Leask, Mathias Pöhling, Ryan Leask,
Mathias Pöhling

SAP xApp Analytics

A practical guide to implementing and using
SAP xApp Analytics

This book fulfills two goals. First, it gives readers a
look at the technology behind building Analytic
Applications within SAP. Second, it gives a business
perspective as to why xApp Analytics are beneficial.
It addresses how SAP meets industry-specific
challenges with various pre-packaged Analytic
applications. Practical examples and the authors'
experiences while working with Analytics are
valuable resources for readers. Readers will also
obtain insight into the future of xApp Analytics.
Other topics include installation, administration,
transporting, and coverage of the Visual Composer.

Learn account determination
techniques for integration
touch-points to SAP Financials

Increase productivity by
automating commonly used
business processes

90 pp., 2006, 68,– Euro / US$ 85.—
ISBN 978-1-59229-110-6

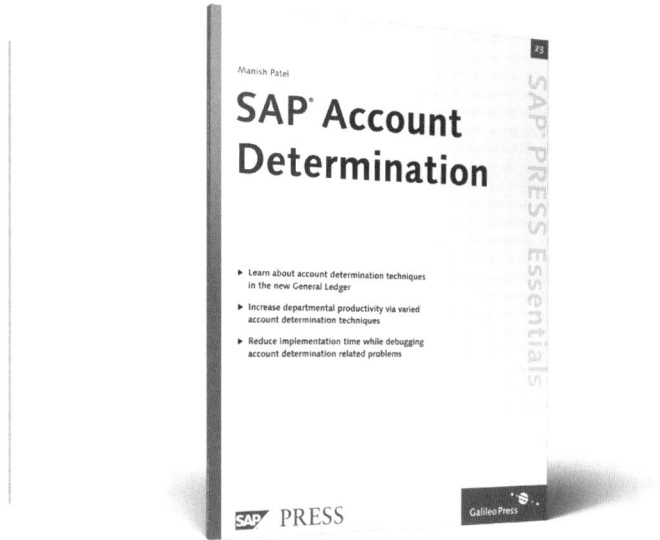

Manish Patel

SAP Account
Determination

▶ Learn about account determination techniques
  in the new General Ledger

▶ Increase departmental productivity via varied
  account determination techniques

▶ Reduce implementation time while debugging
  account determination related problems

SAP PRESS   Galileo Press

SAP Account Determination

www.sap-hefte.de

Manish Patel

SAP Account Determination

SAP PRESS Essentials 23

This Essentials Guide is tightly focused on important
account determination techniques relevant for
different SAP modules. Get clarification of the various
techniques in each module for generating General
Ledger postings. Learn account determination
techniques for modules like MM and SD. With
coverage on AR/AP, tax, and bank transactions, this
Essentials Guide is just the resource you've been
looking for. Save time and effort by learning the ins
and outs of account determination in SAP.

Fully understand invoice verification and its role in SAP MM and FI

Expert advice to optimize this powerful and comprehensive functionality

80 pp., 2006, US$ 85.00/68,– Euro
ISBN 1-59229-083-3

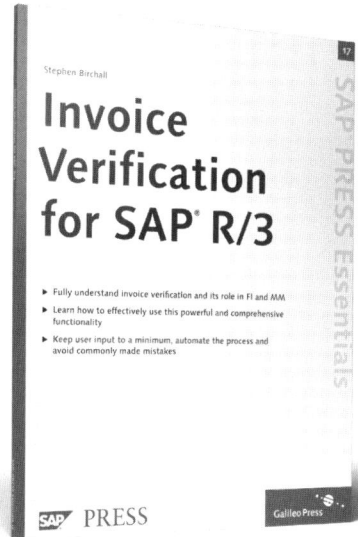

Invoice Verification for SAP R/3

www.sap-hefte.de

Stephen Birchall

Invoice Verification for SAP R/3

SAP PRESS Essentials 17

Regardless of which functional team you belong to, you may find yourself charged with the crucial invoice verification function. This book helps get readers up to speed quickly and effectively. It gives project managers, leaders and team members a rapid and practical introduction to invoice verification, before proceeding to train them on its specific functions, focusing on financial details, configuration and many other important issues.

Demystify production variance analysis for SAP Controlling

Optimize production processes and company performance

Fully leverage your SAP investment by accurately analyzing your company's performance

110 pp., 2006, 68,– Euro / US$ 85.—
ISBN 978-1-59229-109-0

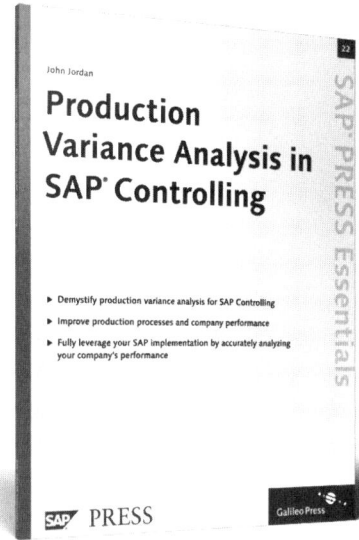

Production Variance Analysis in SAP Controlling

www.sap-hefte.de

John Jordan

Production Variance Analysis in SAP Controlling

SAP PRESS Essentials 25

Learn about plan costs and actual costs and how variances between the two can impact your company's performance. This specific and targeted Essentials Guide shows you how variance analysis can be used to analyze your company's processes and determine how they can be enhanced to improve the bottom line. Keep costs down and processes optimized in your company by using this Essentials Guide.

An integrated approach to analyzing liquidity

How to perform successful cash accounting in SAP R/3

In-depth details on exact cash flow planning using SAP BW and SAP SEM

88 pp., 2006
68,00 Euro, 85,00 US$
ISBN 1-59229-070-1

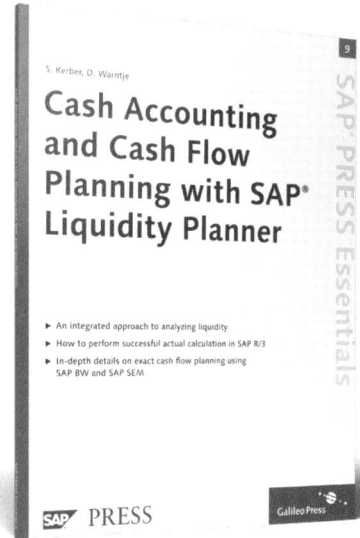

S. Kerber, D. Warntje

Cash Accounting
and Cash Flow
Planning with SAP®
Liquidity Planner

▶ An integrated approach to analyzing liquidity
▶ How to perform successful actual calculation in SAP R/3
▶ In-depth details on exact cash flow planning using
   SAP BW and SAP SEM

SAP PRESS

Galileo Press

Cash Accounting and Cash Flow Planning with SAP Liquidity Planner

www.sap-hefte.de

S. Kerber, D. Warntje

Cash Accounting and Cash Flow Planning with SAP Liquidity Planner

SAP PRESS Essentials 9

This SAP PRESS Essentials guide teaches you how to optimize your use of SAP for liquidity calculation and planning. SAP Liquidity Planner consists of SAP Actual Calculation (cash accounting) and SAP BW/ SEM. The first part of the book describes how you can successfully implement cash accounting in SAP R/3. Each relevant area of SAP Actual Calculation, from the technical settings (via customization) through to the liquidity analysis processes is described in great detail. The subsequent sections provide you with a fundamental introduction to reporting and planning using SAP BW/SEM. The last chapter concludes with details of an exclusive workaround that enables you to perform liquidity planning and reporting without SAP BW/SEM.